TRANSCENDING RACIAL BARRIERS

TRANSCENDING RACIAL BARRIERS

BARRIERS

Toward a Mutual Obligations Approach

Michael O. Emerson
George Yancey

OXFORD
UNIVERSITY PRESS

2011

OXFORD
UNIVERSITY PRESS

Oxford University Press, Inc., publishes works that further
Oxford University's objective of excellence
in research, scholarship, and education.

Oxford New York
Auckland Cape Town Dar es Salaam Hong Kong Karachi
Kuala Lumpur Madrid Melbourne Mexico City Nairobi
New Delhi Shanghai Taipei Toronto

With offices in
Argentina Austria Brazil Chile Czech Republic France Greece
Guatemala Hungary Italy Japan Poland Portugal Singapore
South Korea Switzerland Thailand Turkey Ukraine Vietnam

Published by Oxford University Press, Inc.
198 Madison Avenue, New York, New York 10016
www.oup.com

Oxford is a registered trademark of Oxford University Press

Library of Congress Cataloging-in-Publication Data
Emerson, Michael O., 1965-
Transcending racial barriers : toward a mutual obligations approach /
Michael O. Emerson, George Yancey.
p. cm.
Includes bibliographical references and index.
ISBN 978-0-19-974268-4 (hardback : alk. paper)
ISBN 978-0-19-974269-1 (pbk. : alk. paper)
1. Racism—United States—History. 2. United States—Race relations.
3. Conflict management—United States. I. Yancey, George A., 1962– II. Title.
E184.A1E553 2010
305.800973—dc22   2009050106

To those who sacrifice for a better world

CONTENTS

ACKNOWLEDGEMENTS

This book was a collaborative project in every way, and the authors thank each other for a spirited working environment. We are thankful to the students and professors who read and commented on earlier versions of this book. We are grateful to our editor, James Cook, for his guidance in this project. Moreover, we continue to stand in awe of the ability of copy editors, who transform our broken prose into clear communication. Our production editor, Brian Desmond, has done his job admirably.

The goal of this book is to propose a specific, workable solution to racial division. Some would say it takes a rather big ego (or in our case, two egos) to even entertain offering a solution to centuries-long racial division. Yet, rather than being driven by ego, we engaged in this project because of our belief that sociology, and social science more broadly, must move beyond identifying and explaining social realities. It must also use that knowledge to devise workable solutions to vexing social problems. Too often in courses on race and ethnicity (ours included), ninety percent or more of the time is devoted to identifying the issues. Perhaps at the end of the course, for a class or two, discussion moves to possible solutions. To the students we have talked to, this imbalance in focus makes the solutions seem almost like an afterthought, and of limited importance. We wanted to overcome that imbalance by writing an entire book dedicated to proposing a workable solution, one that takes into account the breadth of previously offered solutions and draws the best from them.

We are humbled in writing this book. So much work has come before us, and so many others have enlightened us, by seeing behind the obvious. So many people have sacrificed for the goal of overcoming the negatives of this relatively modern invention called race. We are truly indebted.

TRANSCENDING RACIAL BARRIERS

PART I

WHERE WE ARE

※

ONE

INTRODUCTION

It was supposed to be simple: buy a minivan and go back home. One of the authors (Emerson) was responding to a newspaper ad for a minivan for sale. The couple listing the vehicle lived in Fort Bend County, a racially diverse suburban county of Houston, Texas. More specifically, though, the couple lived in a largely white, middle-class subdivision that we will call Dove Trail. Like many suburban areas, Fort Bend County is composed of a series of neighborhoods called subdivisions, ranging in size from a few hundred homes to, in Dove Trail's case, many thousands of homes. Although Fort Bend County is racially diverse, its subdivisions tend not to be.

Using an online map, Emerson traveled from his home to the Dove Trail subdivision. There he met the husband selling the minivan. Asking questions, Emerson learned that this man was a mechanical engineer and took care of his minivan with the type of precision one would associate with an engineer. He had kept careful records of each oil change (every three months, without fail) and every service, complete with the cost, date, and location of the service. Average miles per gallon were calculated and recorded for every tank of gas. The detail was helpful and comforting, and the minivan drove wonderfully. After some more questions, the deal was sealed with a handshake and a check.

At that point, making small talk, Emerson asked the man about the Dove Trail subdivision, noting that it seemed very nice. "We love it here," the man responded, "great amenities, wonderful neighbors, and the location is what we wanted. But to be honest, we do have real concerns about the high school they have us zoned to. Too many minorities, you know."

Having just made a sale, he seemed to now view Emerson as a friend (and of the same race), someone to whom he could tell what he really thought. He continued:

> Jenkins High School is just not a school for this neighborhood's kids. We've invested too much in our homes to have our property values brought down by having to send our kids to a high school full of minorities who don't much care about education. To be blunt, we are going to have to get that changed, but we are hopeful that will happen before our kids get to high school. The neighbors here are in agreement not only that we need the change, but that we can get it done in the next few years. Believe me, you wouldn't want your kids in that jungle.

Upon returning home, Emerson looked up data on the high school in question. He found that, at that time, the racial makeup of the school was about 40 percent African American, 15 percent Asian, 20 percent Hispanic, and 25 percent Anglo. The school had four magnet programs, including a medical one and one in engineering, that helped increase the diversity of the school. Most Asian students, for example, did not live in the Jenkins zone but attended Jenkins through the magnet programs. The school seemed to be high performing relative to most schools in the Houston region and, being only about five years old, was relatively new. On the surface, the data did not seem to match this man's stated perceptions.

Fast forward two years . . .

It had been bubbling for many years, but on this night, it boiled over. The occasion was a seemingly ho-hum event, a school-district rezoning community forum. Much like Jenkins High School, the Fort Bend School District is racially and ethnically diverse: about 30 percent of the students are African American, 22 percent Asian, 25 percent Hispanic, and 23 percent Anglo, with more than ninety languages and dialects spoken in the homes of students (http://www.fortbend.k12.tx.us/diversity/breakdown.cfm).

It is also one of the nation's fifty-five largest school districts and is growing rapidly. At the time of this writing, it has about seventy thousand students and eleven high schools. But with the rapid population growth of the area, new schools are added nearly every year, which means that altering attendance boundaries, called rezoning, is common. Rezoning means that where students in the district attend school can change from year to year, even if they do not move. Rezoning is not ideal and must be handled with care. Add racial diversity to the mix, and rezoning can become quite a contested issue.

So the school district, like many growing school districts, has a set policy for handling rezoning. The Fort Bend School District hires an outside consulting firm that specializes in providing enrollment projections, selecting the sites for new schools, and realigning attendance zones. Once that firm completes its initial work, it produces several possible sites and attendance zone–realignment strategies, keeping in mind the districts' priorities: use "natural" boundaries (such as rivers and roads) for attendance boundaries, reduce overcrowded schools, favor neighborhood schools, and support academic achievement. The firm's representatives then meet with the school board and superintendent in a series of about five workshops to produce—again, with the districts priorities in mind—one agreed upon recommendation.

At that point it can get interesting, because community input is sought through community forums. It was at the community forum that Emerson attended that racial tensions that had been brewing in the district for many years came to the surface. The issue in question was relieving overcrowding at Jenkins High School. The recommended solution was to alter the attendance zone by splitting in half the Dove Trail subdivision. Those living on the east side of the subdivision would remain at Jenkins; those living on the west side (where the engineer lived) would all attend Smith, a high school a few miles to the west of the Dove Trail subdivision, which had room for more students (and an already much higher percentage of white pupils).

The change in attendance zones would relieve overcrowding but also (a) reduce the racial diversity of both Jenkins and Smith, and (b) mean that students on either side of the main road in Dove Trail would attend different schools. At the community forum, residents of all hues and backgrounds were livid, except for those who lived on the west side of Dove Trail.

The community forum is run by the firm that is hired to do the demographic projections and rezoning plans. School board members and the superintendent are not present. At the beginning of the forum, those in attendance were told again about the rezoning plans (all those in the district had already received e-mails and mailings about the rezoning). After the new plans were clearly explained, the attendees were told that their comments were welcomed and valued. No responses to their comments would be given, they were told, but everything said by microphone or through note cards would be recorded and considered by the superintendent and school board before they made their final decisions on the rezoning.

Parents lined up to speak. For perhaps five minutes, the comments and questions were calm. But then the dialogue escalated. Several white parents, almost all from the east side of Dove Trail, lined up first. For at least thirty minutes, they discussed in much detail how the proposed rezoning would bring down their property values, would subject their children to an inferior education, and would even mean people would move from the east side of Dove Trail to the west side. As one impassioned parent from the east side said, "If you go ahead with rezoning as you propose here, you are sentencing the east side of Dove Trail to be a ghost town! We don't want our kids at Jenkins, and we won't accept it!"

At that, several African American and Latino parents lined up. The comments turned from a focus on the rezoning implications to a focus on the meanings of the white parents' comments. One Latino parent said that he did not understand why the white parents thought Jenkins such a bad place to be. Turning to the white parents, he said, "Do you not like us? Have we done something to you? Do you think we do not care about the education of our children?" An African American parent was next:

> I have sat here and listened to the residents of Dove Trail talk as if the rest of us are not here. I have heard them say how much they don't want their children at Jenkins. We know exactly why you don't want your children at Jenkins. It's because my children and the previous gentleman's children attend Jenkins! You don't want your children going to school with people you think are inferior! My husband and I both have college degrees, we both have professional, well-paying careers. But still we are not good enough for you! You have stood here, and person after person, you have insulted us, you have belittled us! I hope you are proud of your behavior, because I don't know if I will ever get over what I have seen here tonight.

We could go on. It got worse. White parents saying they were appalled that they were being accused of racism. Since when, they asked, did caring about the education of their children make them racist? Black and Hispanic parents countered, with one saying, "If it looks like a duck, quacks like a duck, it is a duck, a racist duck!"

Through it all, the school district representatives up front—the "hired guns"—simply sat there and took notes, occasionally reminding those in attendance that they should keep their comments focused on the rezoning issue, and that they were not there to answer questions, only to record the comments. After the scheduled two hours, though parents continued to line up to speak, the representatives announced the meeting had concluded, thanked everyone for their participation, and said that if those in attendance had further comments, they should write them on the note cards and leave them in the boxes provided.

Perhaps a month later, the finalized rezoning plan was announced. The school board and superintendent—all white except for a woman of Indian descent—approved a plan that was exactly the same as the proposed plan: splitting Dove Trail in half. But it was also announced that this would be a temporary solution, as funding had been approved for an additional high school, which would open within three years . . . in Dove Trail. This meant that the students of Dove Trail would be re-united, in their own high school. And the wishes of the engineer and his neighbors living in Dove Trail, who a few years earlier had voiced their desire and had planned to keep Dove Trail kids from having to attend Jenkins, were fulfilled.

What has become of Jenkins High School? The school has gone from 25 percent white five years ago to less than ten percent white. When the new Dove Trail high school opens in a few months, there will be almost no white students left at Jenkins. There will be sub-stantially fewer Asian students as well, given that their number has already declined and that it was announced that at least two of the magnet programs at Jenkins will be moving to other high schools. Jenkins, then, has become less racially diverse over time. It is now populated almost exclusively by African American and Latino students.

A week before writing this chapter—and three years since the community forum—Emerson was exercising at the local YMCA, where he overheard two African American men talking. Both men have children attending Jenkins. Recalling the rezoning issue, they clearly were not happy. One remarked, "Those white folks are straight up racist, the way they ramrod what they want through that school board." To which the other man replied, "They wouldn't want their precious children going to school with our children. No, man, that might bring them down." The other man responded in turn, "The system is straight up stacked against us, and white folks just keep walkin' 'round like we got no problems. They know what they've done, and yet they still callin' themselves Christians. It ain't right, it ain't right."

Clearly, racial problems in this school district continue to stew and undoubtedly will again boil over. The school district's solutions for dealing with racial diversity and racial alienation as they seek to best educate the district's children are not working. In fact, they are making things worse.

This book is about the fact that most of our proposed solutions to racial issues do not work. More importantly, it is about proposing an alternative way to think about addressing such issues, what we call the mutual-obligations approach.

Take, for example, the racial issues discussed above. What if a different approach were used? Applying the mutual-obligations approach, let us suggest an alternative. We won't go into great detail about the approach here, as we spend the second half of the book doing so. But to introduce where this book ultimately is going, we briefly outline an alternative approach for the specific instance of better addressing racial divisions when attempting school-district rezoning. Don't be fooled by the specificity of this example. We are merely applying in a local context our approach designed to address racial divisions nationally.

The school board should first recognize that racial division, stereotypes, and racism are real and are affecting their district. They celebrate that they are diverse (the district's Web site says so!). But they are not integrated, even if they do have children of diverse backgrounds attending the same schools. Rather than essentially ignoring racial problems, they should devise a way to address them head on.

We know that rezoning in this school district is an almost yearly event. So rather than including parents at the end of the rezoning process, when all they can do is express their agreement or dismay, the district should include parents up front, letting them play a significant role in the entire process. Specifically, the district should form parent-led committees—its members elected—that are specifically charged with proposing their own plans for altering attendance boundaries in a fair, equitable way. Regardless of the racial composition of the district, the committees should have equal numbers of each major racial group (if there are strong ethnic differences, as, say, between Mexicans and Colombians, then there should be representation from each ethnic group). Given the process that these committees will engage in, as described below, the district will have to provide trained facilitators to guide the parents through the meetings and rezoning process.

Before these groups begin working on rezoning issues, there should be a gathering where the group members begin learning about each other as people. At the second meeting, they should talk about what they hope for in their children's education. What do they value? Does the racial diversity of the school matter? Why? Is participation in extracurricular activities part of a high-quality education?

At the third meeting, racial issues should be explicitly discussed. Too often race is the unspoken, the assumed, or the ignored. Based on the prior meeting, were there any racial differences in what people considered a high-quality education? No matter the answer, it should be discussed. No matter what occurs at this meeting, consensus should be sought—what can all the committee members agree upon? These agreements will be vital for moving past standstills in the rezoning process.

Beginning with the fourth meeting, the committees should be presented with the restrictions within which they must devise their rezoning plans. This would include budget restrictions, the preference by nearly all parents to limit bussing where possible, and the district's desire to maximize racial diversity within schools. Armed with this information, information on demographic projections, and knowledge of approved new schools, they should set about the task of rezoning.

How they do this matters. Power differentials and mistrust must be minimized by having parents of various neighborhoods (racially distinct neighborhoods, at least in the school district we are discussing here) work separately to come up with the plan they think is best. Of course, they will be biased toward the children and youth in their own neighborhood, and that is exactly the desired outcome.

Once that process is complete, each neighborhood subcommittee comes back to the larger group to present their plans. They will be different, and biased. This is to be expected. But because they spent the time getting to know each other as people and discussing what they all value and share in common in excellent education, they can proceed to the important next steps without mistrust and accusations immediately beginning to fly.

The next step would be for each subcommittee to take the other subcommittee's proposals and produce a rezoning plan that best balances each of the separate plans. They would each then bring their new, more balanced plan to the whole committee. Differences would remain, but the process would ensure they will be smaller than the differences in the original proposals.

Now the real negotiations begin. The committee must arrive at one plan, one that integrates the "balanced plans" each subcommittee has brought back to the group. They must come to complete (or nearly complete) agreement on the one best plan, of course recognizing that though no one plan is best for everybody individually, one plan is best for everybody collectively. Once they have found that one, that is the plan they will present to the school board. The school board should be held to that plan; if they feel they must make changes, they must do so in consultation with the parent groups.

To keep all in the school district informed, the elected committee should write a letter to the people of the district explaining the process and why the selected plan is the best one for the community, given the constraints they must work within. It should be signed by all the committee members.

We could go into more detail, and we can debate whether parts of our proposed solution should be altered, but our goal here is merely to make a point, which is that there is a better way to address racial division, alienation, and inequality. Notice some of the components we have suggested, and will discuss in later chapters: initiating inter-racial communication under controlled conditions, listening to each other, acknowledging and defining racial problems, searching for a critical core all agree upon, giving voice to cultural uniqueness, recognizing and incorporating individual and group interest, and devising ways that allow for negotiation of these individual and group interests to produce a solution to which all can agree. We call this the mutual-obligations approach. It is something like the process in marital counseling, but on a much larger scale. This larger scale makes solutions more complicated and requires using more steps and relying on more principles.

Race in the United States—In But a Few Pages

Race clearly matters in many, many aspects of life. We can summarize this by saying that the United States is a *racialized society*. What do we mean by a racialized society? We have spent the first few pages introducing some of its manifestations. But we can define it as a society wherein race matters profoundly for differences in life experiences, life opportunities, and social relationships. It is a society "that allocates differential economic, political, social, and even psychological rewards to groups along racial lines; lines that are socially constructed" (Bonilla-Silva 1997: 474). We can also look at it as a society that has institutionalized favoritism for some groups over others. Based on volumes of research, statistics, and studies, U.S. society is racialized in at least the following areas: health, death, employment, marriage, occupations, life expectancy, crime, personal and social identity, advertising, names, education, residential neighborhoods, auto loan rates, socioeconomic and spatial mobility, consumerism, respect, expectations, music, religion, cost of products, mortgage rates, history, TV watching, wealth, property values, politics, entrepreneurship, access to high-quality affordable products, self-esteem, product mark-up prices, environmental pollution and hazardous waste, social networks, high school and college lunch tables, and comfortable access to places around the nation.

We grow weary of these issues and debates. Out of frustration, we become indifferent to the whole thing. It's complicated, it's messy, it's risky—best to just avoid it when possible. Thus, much of the racial dilemmas that keep emerging in our society become mere background noise that we try to ignore. But deep down, we know there is something better and that we ought to pursue it. We might even call it a yearning. Wouldn't it be something if finally, after hundreds of years, we could reach it?

This book has one main goal: *to work toward a solution to racial division, racial inequality, racial alienation, and the racialized society*. By "racial division" we mean that socially created racial groups are physically, socially, and psychologically separated from one another. By "racial inequality" we mean the very real economic, political, and other forms of unequal access or possession by racial group. By "racial alienation" we mean the profound distrust between racial groups. And all of these are part of the racialized society. We use racial division, inequality, and alienation almost interchangeably throughout the book not because they mean same thing but because they are all core components of the problem.

To even sniff at a solution, we must begin with a basic understanding of what it means to be part of a socially created racial group, because this racial-group membership, it turns out, causes quite a few problems.

On Being White

From a white person's perspective, it is not easy to be white these days.[1] First, any time the topic of race comes up, it feels to whites like they are the objects of blame, anger, misperception, and ridicule. Whites are often put on the defensive. Second, given programs such as affirmative action, it also seems as if preferential treatment is given to anyone who is not white. In this vein, it might look like society is racialized, but in the sense that it favors nonwhites. "Why can't we just get over this race thing and live as Americans?" whites in the United States often think. "Why does it have to be so complicated? Sure there may be a few racist people, but they are but a tiny percentage. Society is open to any and all who want to put the time and effort into achieving their dreams. So let's stop talking about race and living in the past; let's move on and get to eating some of the fruits of the American way of life."[2]

To be white in the United States does come with privileges, despite the real drawbacks mentioned above. Scholars who study what it means to be white describe that privilege in three dimensions:[3]

1. **White Structural Advantage**: Whites occupy the location of dominance—politically, economically, culturally, and numerically—within the racial hierarchy. They disproportionately control influence of political parties, the legal system, government-controlled institutions, industry and business, and so on. These structural advantages provide privileges to whites, where privilege is defined as unearned benefits deriving merely from having a white identity. This advantage can be seen in everyday situations and at institutional levels. For example, whites can easily purchase movies, literature, or greeting cards depicting whites; they can ignore the experiences, writings, or ideas of racial and ethnic minorities without penalty; they are assumed to be middle class, law abiding, and well meaning, unless they prove otherwise (and they will have to work at proving it); they have the ability to set laws and policies (in part because an overwhelming majority of elected officials are white). As well, they have the power to decide who is white and who is not; the power to interpret what is a racial problem and what is not, who is uppity and who is not, who gets into the country and who does not; and the ability to implement housing policies that favor their racial group and influence the development of educational curriculum that emphasizes Western history and social experiences.

2. **White Normativity**: Structural advantage facilitates white normativity—the normalization of whites' cultural practices, ideologies, and location within the racial hierarchy such that how whites do things, their understandings about life, society, and the world, and their dominant social location over other racial groups are accepted *as just how things are.* Anything that diverges from this norm is deviant.

Whites are privileged because, unlike nonwhites, they do not need to justify their way of doing or being. Instead, the burden for change is on the perceived deviants. Although white culture has many variations (compare, for example, rural, Republican, NASCAR-loving, catfish-eatin' Southern whites, and wealthy, Democratic, opera-loving, quiche-eating Bostonian whites), there remains an overarching normativity, a "configuration of [racial] practice which embodies the currently accepted answer to the problem of legitimacy of [whiteness]' . . . that secures the dominant position of whites" (A. Lewis 2004). That is, whites uphold practices and beliefs that sustain their dominant position in the racial hierarchy. Thus, the practices and understandings of whites are normalized, and their interests affirmed.

   3. **White Transparency** is defined as "the tendency of whites not to think . . . about norms, behaviors, experiences, or perspectives that are white-specific" (Flagg 1993: 953). Whites typically lack a racial consciousness. Most whites are unaware that they are "raced" and that their race has real consequences for their lives. Rather, they believe that they earn what they get and that their achievements are nearly all based on individual effort, talent, and creativity. Whites often believe they are cultureless; it doesn't "mean" anything to be white, they may think. They often think that only other groups have distinctive cultures and ways of being. Thus, whites find it difficult to explain what it means to be white. In fact, they typically find it uncomfortable, and even offensive, to be asked. This is white transparency. Given this transparency, a white person is seen simply as an American, or perhaps as someone who has an ethnicity and eats some special foods on holidays. White transparency is a powerful tool for maintaining privilege because of its elusive nature. How can one challenge white privilege if there is no such thing as white culture or white practices? White transparency is also why whites can feel like they are fully under attack for little reason, and why they may feel that society is set up against them. To be white means, in part, that one does not see the advantages garnered from being white, so any threat against taken-for-granted ways of life is indeed threatening and feels unjustified.

   These three dimensions of whiteness—white structural advantage, white normativity, and white transparency—work together to sustain white hegemony; that is, whites' position at the top. Importantly, these dimensions can produce dominance without whites' feeling like it is true (though almost anyone who is not white believes it to be true).

On Being "Black"

To be "black" means, in part, to realize that the United States is racialized. How much people will feel and experience this depends on age, class, location, and other factors. But scholarship shows, repeatedly, that the negative effects of the racialized nature of the United States are experienced most forcefully by African Americans.[4] In fact, the experience of African Americans as a group becomes that to which others' experiences are often compared. This has resulted in parallel realities for African Americans and majority-group members, which we see not only in the different economic, educational, health and status outcomes but also in the differential outlook of African Americans on a wide variety of racial issues.

At the same time, being black in America is under constant negotiation and is always changing. For example, what does it mean to be black in a nation whose president is black? Is that the end of racial struggle? Is the election of an African American president perhaps merely an anomaly? Or does Barack Obama's election means something in between these extremes? It is too soon to know, but as time passes, the meaning of Obama's election will be better understood, and it will have implications for what it means to be black in the United States.

One thing that has remained unchanged with the election of Barack Obama is that being racially mixed means you are not white. Barack Obama's mother was white, his father black. But no one ever suggests he is a white man. At times, especially early on in his candidacy, there were discussions of whether he was black enough, but ultimately, the centuries-old way of classifying people has continued: part black equals all black.

On Being "Neither White nor Black"

One of the great conundrums of American society, especially given the massive growth of immigration since 1965, is what it means to live in the racialized society of the United States but be neither black nor white. Talk about identity issues—both at the individual and group levels. If you are from Vietnam, for example, and have moved to the United States, are you Vietnamese American, Asian American, both, or something else? And once that is determined, what does it mean to be that? Should you operate as a unique racial group, apart from blacks and whites, fighting for political favors and establishing identity?

Should you attempt to assimilate into one or another "native" racial group? If so, what will this entail? And what will it take to ultimately be seen as fully American rather than as an outsider?

The tens of millions of Americans who are neither black nor white are growing at a pace never before seen in the United States, and racial negotiation is occurring at lightning speed. Sometimes these groups align with African Americans, to comprise a super-minority. At others times evidence suggests these groups align with whites to form an expanding majority. Many times, members of these groups align with neither blacks nor whites and instead are defining their own interests, such as over the importance of immigration, border issues, and family unification.

Despite much uncertainty, evidence seems to suggest that people and groups who are neither black nor white attempt to avoid racial problems and work hard to avoid being caught at the bottom end of the racialized society (Bonilla-Silva 2003, Yancey 2003b). For most groups, this entails doing so on their own terms, as a unique and respected racial or ethnic group, distinct from white and black Americans.

The Race/Race Relations/Racial Inequality Dilemma—or, Why We Are Writing This Book

Racialized outcomes have failed to evaporate over time. This is not merely due to neglect. We have seen continual attempts to find programs and remedies that address racial hostility and alienation. Yet the persistent racialization in our society shows that these attempts continue to have, at best, mixed results for dealing with our unremitting racial problems. It is said that insanity is doing the same thing over and over again with the expectation of a different result. We need to take a new direction when tackling issues of race. Past efforts have failed to significantly alter the basic dynamic of continued racial hostility, misunderstandings, and inequality, from which so many continue to suffer. To reiterate, the purpose of this book is to attempt to chart such a new path, one we call the **mutual-obligations** approach.

We will do so by first briefly examining our racial history, what has been proposed and tried, and why we have failed (chapters 2–5). Clearly, there is a missing piece in the solutions that have so far been proposed to address racialization in the United States. That missing piece, we will argue, is the failure of social reformers to take into consideration a comprehensive understanding of in-group preferences in the context of working toward common goals. Put most bluntly, until we can incorporate in-group selfishness, we cannot overcome racial division, inequality, and alienation. In the second half of the book (chapters 6 through 10), we shall attempt to outline how we might go about doing so.

TWO

HOW DID WE GET HERE?

Social situations can only rarely be understood without considering the current and historical context. A parent berating a child may seem cruel—until we learn that the adult is trying to teach the child to look out for cars before crossing a street. This scolding may end up saving the child's life. In a similar vein, when we see a man giving his lover flowers we may think he is a caring lover—until we find out that he is an abuser who is trying to win his girlfriend back and thus perpetuate a cycle of abuse. Snap judgments are often wrong. To avoid misinterpretation, we must consider the current and historical context of the social situation.

Race relations in the United States cannot be understood by looking at our contemporary racial situation. Few individuals will dispute the fact that issues of race have had profound effects in our society historically. Even a cursory look at our past reveals issues of slavery, extermination, labor abuse, and discrimination that are inexorably linked to our racialized society. Political and legal reforms have reduced the effects of this overt type of white supremacy, but the results of historical racism continue to affect the present. Consider just a brief thought experiment to see why. If twenty years ago we gave you ten dollars and gave another person ten thousand dollars, today that gap in money would either remain or, even more likely, be larger. Time does not bring equality; the past affects the present. Consequently, understanding the link between historical racism and its contemporary forms is essential in our search for solutions to the modern racial problems plaguing society. Eliminating the economic, and even cultural, effects of this historical racism is a key challenge that looms in our society.

In this chapter we briefly examine the historical establishment of racial alienation. We look at the development of white supremacy in the United States. We then explore how this overt form of racism eventually morphed into the indirect institutional racism we see today. This leads us into an exploration of theories of contemporary racism that attempt to to explain society's transition from the problems connected to overt racism to the issues produced in modern racialization. Finally, we illustrate how these modern forms of racialization continue to affect society.

The Development of White Supremacy in the United States

Often we hear from students and people in the community that racial favoritism (and the racial inequality that results) is innate, simply humans beings humans. But systems of racial privilege are relatively new in the larger scope of human history. Social oppression based on human groupings has always been a part of our societies, but until relatively recently this oppression has not generally been linked to notions of physical distinctions. If we define racism as *creating or maintaining racial group inequality and justifying that inequality*, then racism may not have begun to develop until the emergence of the Atlantic Slave trade (Fredrickson 1971, W. J. Wilson 1973) in the seventeenth century. Before that time, religion, geography, and culture were the criteria by which social groups decided to oppress each other.

The early Africans were imported into the New World as indentured servants (Pinkney 2000, Ringer 1983). In many ways they were not treated very differently from the European indentured servants who also were brought into the English colonies, although they were perceived as being inferior to whites (Jordan 1968, Ringer 1983, Spickard 1989). Members of both races were treated as indentured servants for three to seven years and then released from further obligation. They had, in a very real sense, earned their freedom.

However, as the Southern economy became more agrarian based, the need grew, at least in the eyes of the landowners, for individuals who would work as indentured servants indefinitely—that is, who would be enslaved for all of their lives, and whose children would inherit that status. Political obligations made the conversion of European indentured servants into lifelong slaves an impossibility, and Native Americans could too easily escape and blend in with their tribes. But there were no protections for Africans (Handlin 1957). Thus, the stage was set for the development of the chattel slavery that would dominate the American South.

However, the use of Africans, but not Europeans, as lifelong slaves required philosophical justification. This justification was soon found in a social construction of racial differences wherein blacks were seen as biologically inferior to whites. Africans were conceptualized as simple-minded and in need of care of by the superior white race (Elkin 1976, Jordan 1968). This conceptualization led to the ideas that blacks naturally belonged in a subservient position to whites. The development of such stereotypes of Africans and African Americans is an important part of the construction of the white supremacy ideology that dominated U.S. culture for many centuries.

Although white supremacy was created in the slave trade involving blacks, it would be a mistake to limit the effects of this doctrine to the treatment of Africans and African Americans. This type of ideology was also important in justifying the removal of Native Americans from the lands they inhabited. White supremacy held that Europeans better understood how to use the land than did Native peoples (Berkhofer 1979, O'Neill 2002, Washburn 1975). Thus, notions of white supremacy ideologically fueled the initial attempts at extermination and the later internment of Native Americans. White supremacy was the ideology that undergirded the displacement of Native Americans from their ancestral lands through the Indian Removal Act of 1824.[1] Furthermore, white supremacy could be seen in the way Native American culture was generally perceived. Historically (and perhaps currently), white Americans have believed European American culture to be superior to Native culture. This belief led to efforts to force Native Americans to adopt a European American based agrarian lifestyle through the Dawes Act[2] and to efforts of white social workers and missionaries to remove Native American children from their homes and raise them as culturally white.[3] Given such efforts, it is little wonder that many tribes have lost or must search for many or most of the key aspects of their Native American culture, such as language, religion, and social customs.

This type of white supremacy was also firmly in place as European Americans encountered Hispanics. After winning the war with Mexico, Hispanic citizens were given a second-class societal position as a conquered people. The ideology of white supremacy clearly spelled out that individuals of Hispanic heritage were not fit for leadership positions in a predominately white society; thus, Hispanic Americans were relegated to low-paying, difficult work.[4] Because they were relegated to menial work, stereotypes about their work ethic and intelligence developed. Hispanics were seen as laid back, unambitious, and unable to handle professional jobs because of their perceived intellectual inferiority. This perception about the biological origins of the occupational failure of Hispanics persisted in spite of the clear racial discrimination they continued to face. In this way European Americans were able to maintain the top social and cultural position they enjoyed in a society dominated by the ideology of white supremacy.

This ideology of white supremacy was solidly in place when Asians began immigrating into the United States in large numbers. It is an ideology that counsels mistrust of those who are clearly not European. This mistrust led to the passing of overtly racist laws against Asians and Asian Americans, such as the Chinese Exclusion Act[5] and the Alien Land Law Act of California.[6] Such legislation was passed based on the idea that Asians had to be stopped from taking over the U.S. economy. Notions of white supremacy have contributed to the stereotyping of Asians as conniving and dishonest (R. G. Lee 1999, Manchester-Boddy 1970, Spickard 1989) as Asian Americans could not be conceived of as being equal to European Americans. It is not an accident that Pearl Harbor set into motion the legal mechanisms that ended with the internment of Japanese Americans, but not German Americans.[7] Asian Americans have been consistently seen as devious foreigners who are not a part of U.S. society. This perception is fed by the white supremacist notion of what is acceptable and what is not, and it becomes easy to stigmatize a culture and people with non-European roots. Historically, this stigmatization occurred in spite of the considerable efforts Asian Americans, and other nonwhites, made to abide by the economic and social norms of the United States.

Given the predominance of white supremacist ideology in the United States, it is not surprising that some of the earliest advocates of civil rights did not even fully challenge that doctrine. For example, some of the early abolitionists did not dispute the supposed inferiority of Africans and African Americans, and even argued that a separate colony should be established for blacks so that the "civilized" whites could be protected (Fredrickson 1971). Such efforts generally failed to obtain full civil rights for people of color since these efforts accepted the premise that whites are the superior racial group. However, later civil rights efforts concentrated on debunking the racial stereotypes used to justify the oppressive racial hierarchy. Such stereotypes had become so pervasive that they were simply seen as God-created truths by most whites and many others. Knowing they must find a way to counteract such all-pervasive views, civil rights activists used a variety of ways to demonstrate that people of color had the same abilities, experiences, feelings, strengths, and weaknesses that whites did. By doing so, these activists were able to argue that people of color were as fully human as whites and deserve the same rights as whites. This logic buttressed the development of the 1964 and 1968 Civil Rights Acts and the 1965 Voting Rights Act. This legislation help ensure that people of color would not have to face the overtly racist laws and segregation that had developed under the regime of white superiority.

The activists who helped create modern civil rights legislation were successful in more than just the development of this new legislation. They were also part of a social movement that challenged the ideological core of white supremacy. Since the development of modern civil rights legislation, studies have found a steady decline in white support for the notion that European Americans are inherently superior to other racial groups (Kluegel 1990, Schuman et al. 1997). What has been termed "old-fashioned" racism has fallen into disrepute in the major sectors of U.S. society. Today we have not only laws insisting that European Americans have no greater rights than other racial groups, but also a good deal of social support for such laws.

In some ways the goals of the modern civil rights movement have been achieved. We have rules and laws that negate attempts to enforce the ideology of white supremacy. Furthermore, few people openly support overt racism. Yet, as we recognize these achievements, we note the unexpected outcome: these accomplishments have not ended racial strife, nor have they eliminated institutional racism. They have, however, led many individuals—generally majority-group members—to believe that we have eliminated the problems of racism in our society. This assertion has produced what many social theorists have called modern forms of racism. Understanding these modern forms of racism is critical if we are going to perceive why racial problems persist in our society.

Modern Forms of Racism

Since the development of the modern civil rights movement, adherence to the ideology of white supremacy has been deeply stigmatized.

However, this does not mean that our society is less racialized. Rather, what has been called modern racism (McConahay 1986, T. R. Petti-grew 1989) is used to explain the way racial issues have changed and to account for the types of institutional racism we face. During the days of overt white supremacy, people of color generally suffered from direct institutional discrimination. This type of discrimination saw laws and rules intentionally designed to negatively affect people of color (i.e., Jim Crow laws, the Indian Removal Act, the Alien Land Law Act). With the passage of civil rights legislation such intentional efforts became illegal. However, this has not eliminated indirect institutional discrimination, which is the disparate effect of social norms, laws, and rules not overtly intended to negatively affect people of color. The prevalence of indirect institutional discrimination is supported by the emergence of modern forms of racism.

One example of indirect discrimination is the use of social networks to find a prospective employee. Royster (2003) documents the role that families, school officials, and employers play in enabling whites, rather than blacks, to more smoothly transition to good-paying blue-collar employment. She found that the social networks of whites enable them to enjoy more economic success, even if they are not more academically prepared, than their black counterparts. In and of itself, there is nothing inherently racist about using social networks to find a new hire. Waters (1999) documents that one advantage to doing so is that there the person who provides a reference for a potential employee has some accountability. That accountably makes it less likely that they will recommend an inefficient, troublemaking, or crooked worker. However, our social networks tend to be composed of individuals within our own racial group (Fetto 2000, Joyner & Kao 2000, Korgen 2002). Therefore, the people referred to a potential employer are overwhelmingly likely to be of that recommender's and that employer's race.

Of course, it is not an accident that whites are more likely than nonwhites to be in a position to make hiring decisions. Few people would deny that, historically, racism has affected the chances of non-whites to achieve a higher socioeconomic status (SES) and greater occupational success in our society. Because we pass our SES and occupational status to our children and grandchildren (Kalmijn 1994, Rytina 1992), whites have simply been in a better position to pass a higher occupational status to their offspring, who are then more likely to be in a position to hire whites.[8] Clearly, those who are going to hire someone are more likely to be part of the majority group than is a person of color. Thus, the use of social networks will reinforce the superior ability of majority-group members to be hired, even though the application of this hiring technique need not be intended to be racist.

Because using social networks is a hiring technique that is not intended to be racist, yet has substantial negative effects upon people of color, we can look at its use as a good example of indirect institutional discrimination. Social networks illustrate how our racialized society can perpetuate our racial status quo without the use of a white supremacist ideology. Perhaps this is why whites allowed white supremacist ideology to largely die—it is no longer needed to maintain white privilege. The Civil and Voting Rights Acts passed in the 1960s legislate against white supremacist ideology but are nearly silent about other key mechanisms of racial inequality, such as indirect institutional discrimination.

Escaping the label of "racist" is quite important for majority-group members (Gaertner & Dovidio 1986, Kluegel 1990, Krysan 2002, Rosenthal 1980). Just as racial epithets are often fighting words for people of color, so, too, can being called "racist" lead to anger and hostility among majority-group members. Calling a white person "cracker" or "honky" is likely to lead to laughter or a confused stare, but calling that same person "racist" will boil their blood, put them on the defensive, and often lead to heated exchanges. Thus, modern forms of racism do not overtly support white supremacy, yet people of color still must overcome the negative ways racialization impacts their lives.

A common conception of modern racism is termed "colorblind" racism (Bonilla-Silva & Lewis 1999, Carr 1997). This view claims we are a post-racial society, so we should no longer see color, just people. Any attempt to consider race in any fashion is wrong. Proponents conceptualize colorblindness as an extension of the efforts of the modern civil rights movement, which thereby legitimizes the concept (Bennett 1994, Horowitz & Glazov 2003). However, as we explore in the next chapter, unwillingness to recognize the continuing effects of racialization converts colorblindness into the maintenance of an unequal racial status quo.

Aversive or symbolic racism has also been documented as a modernized form of racism (Bobo 1983, Dovidio & Gaertner 1998, McConahay & Hough Jr. 1976, Sears 1988). Such individuals argue that those in the majority group have an incentive to avoid being perceived as racist in a society that has abandoned notions of white supremacy. However, this does not mean that people have removed racially based suspicion or mistrust from their thinking. Rather, they have learned how to avoid revealing such racial hostility. However, there are many issues in our society that contain a racial and a nonracial component. These issues become symbolic to individuals who have a general aversion to racial out-groups. In this way, a white with such racial hostility toward people of color may allow that hostility to emerge in ways that avoid their being charged as racist.

For example, welfare reform is a question that concerns the best way to aid individuals with a lower SES in our society. On the surface, it seems to be exclusively an issue of class. Yet, because of stereotypes that depict people of color misusing our welfare system (Gilens 1995; Peffley, Hurwitz, and Sniderman. 1997; T. Wilson 1996), there is also an important racial component in discussions of welfare. It is a mistake to ignore these components' effect on our understanding of how lower SES individuals should be aided. Clearly, European Americans who mistrust people of color are unlikely to support financial efforts to aid them. If such individuals perceive welfare programs as financial aid for minorities, then they are likely to oppose them. However, they cannot be automatically charged with racist intentions since there are many individuals supporting alterations to the welfare system for reasons that have nothing to do with racial stereotyping. These "nonracist" opponents to welfare may have a generally conservative political orientation that opposes expanded government. Thus the racial hostility found within the symbolic racist is hidden in his/her opposition to people of color on racially ambiguous issues such as welfare.

The effect of such a modern type of racism is that it becomes much more difficult to gather support for programs that may help people of color overcome the effects of institutional and historical racism. Many such programs do not deal with overt types of white supremacy and thus symbolic/aversive racists are free to oppose these programs without the risk of being labeled racist. For social reformers to gain the public support needed to implement measures dealing with institutional racism, they must overcome not only individuals who have nonracial philosophical opposition to such efforts but also those who oppose such programs as a symbol of their aversion to people of color.

Another theory that explains our modern racial attitudes is group-interest theory (Bobo 2000, Bobo, Kluegel, and Smith 1997). This general theoretical framework is built on the assertion that individuals help themselves by supporting public policies that aid members of their social group. The racial status quo aids the majority group rather than racial minorities. Therefore, it is in the interest of majority-group members to support public policies that maintain the current racial situation, while it is in the interest of people of color to attempt to alter the order in our racialized society. Since the majority group has disproportionate power in the United States, their public policy preferences tend to win.

Thus, the support of social policies concerning race is not predicated upon whether the policies are fair or right, but whether those policies work to the betterment of one's social group. But given that justification of such social policies cannot be based upon the discredited white supremacist ideas of the past, new modern justifications have to be used to justify public policies that buttress the racial status quo. Use of the notion of colorblindness is certainly one mechanism that may serve this purpose. However, majority-group members may also point to the failings within minority-group culture as a source of racial inequality (Carr 1997, Ryan 1976), thereby justifying unequal treatment. Such majority-group members may argue that special attempts to aid people of color work against cherished values of the United States (Hochschild 1995, Moynihan 1965), such as individualism and fairness. These majority-group members also argue that attempts to aid people of color are actually illegal, as they create reverse discrimination, holding majority-group members back to promote the interests of people of color (who whites often see as less qualified than themselves) (Bennett 1994, D'souza 1996, Horowitz & Glazov 2003).

Though, undoubtedly, many individuals believe such rationales, the key to group-interest theory is that the desire to maintain the racial advantage is the real source of support. For example, if whites are used to getting their children into selective colleges, they certainly will not eagerly give up such a privilege in the name of racial equality. Efforts to eliminate the effects of indirect institutional discrimination are efforts to alter the racial status quo that majority-group members enjoy. Thus, such efforts have to be resisted by any possible socially acceptable means. If, for some reason, the above justifications were no longer seen in our society as acceptable, then majority-group members would find new philosophical support in alternative arguments. Therefore, advocacy for social reforms that concern indirect institutional discrimination is unlikely to ever find support among majority-group members. But we reiterate that racism, and not the alternative justifications whites may provide, is ultimately the justification given for maintaining a racial system that maintains inequality.

Why are we spending time examining these theories of modern racism? They indicate paths by which our society remains racialized even though support for white supremacy has dramatically declined. To the activists who buttressed the modern civil rights movement, overcoming the poisonous effects of the white supremacist ideology must have seemed like the solution to the continuing racial hostility and injustice in U.S. society. However, the abandonment of this ideology by many failed to eliminate racial hostility and injustice. Rather, the nature and focus of this hostility has changed. Understanding these changes is important if we are to find solutions to contemporary racial problems.

The Continuing Effect of Modern Forms of Racism

The racial hostility in our society no longer depends upon a white supremacist ideology that places European Americans at the top of the racial hierarchy. But European Americans are still at that privileged position in our social system, and modern forms of racism help ensure that they will remain there. On the other hand, people of color seek to alter the racialized social environment that continues to work to their disadvantage. Thus, racial tensions in the United States develop as majority-group members use indirect measures to ensure the racial status quo, while people of color struggle to achieve parity with majority-group members.

Understanding the changing dynamic of racial struggles is important because the issues debated have drastically changed over the past several decades. No highly influential person today attempts to make a case for white supremacy. Even the most conservative and traditionally based arguments proposed today are advanced on the pretext of supporting racial equality.

Fifty years ago, labeling individuals as racist may not have been considered an insult for some majority-group members. Indeed, many majority-group individuals proudly accepted this label, perceiving themselves as defending their race. Today, few individuals would allow themselves to be called a racist without immediately defending themselves. To be a racist carries such stigma that it invites an immediate loss of status if the person so called does not confront the charge. To this end, we can see a difference between modern and historical conflict. Contemporary racial conflict occurs even though the vast majority of the actors have rejected the idea that any racial group is superior to other racial groups.

The question of whether to accept overt racism is dead. What is still unresolved is whether we truly have equality of opportunity among the races today. Have people of color been able to overcome the horrendous racist policies that they have suffered from in the past? Did the Civil Rights and Voting Rights legislation of the 1960s remove the barriers to racial equality? Or is there more work to be done and do more reforms need to occur before we can confidently assert that people of color have gained their rightful place in our society? This new racial conflict is not based in white supremacy but rather on what should we do, if anything, to combat the effects of white supremacy in its historical aftermath. Moreover, although Americans generally agree that we ought to have equality of opportunity, many see it is patently un-American to even consider equality of outcome. This, then, is a point of contention, too.

These are some of the reasons that we prefer to talk about racialization rather than about racism. The concept of racism evokes the old arguments of white supremacy, which, as we have said, are now largely dead. Racialization is about how race continues to affect the lives of Americans even as U.S. society attempts to downplay the importance of race. The term "racist" is often used—incorrectly, we might add— to denote an evil person who seeks to abuse those who are racially different. Racialization can easily occur without the consent or permission of individual persons. Benign neglect, rather than overt malice, is often the friend of the continuing racialization that is a core component of U.S. society.

By examining racialization rather than racism we begin to understand the full effects of modern forms of racism. These modern forms of racism are not overt attempts to oppress those who are different from the majority group. Rather, they are concepts that indicate the insensitivity that majority-group members have toward efforts to eliminate the effects of historical and/or institutional racism. The concept of "racism" that pervades these modern ideas is clearly not the overt hostility of yesteryear. Rather, it is the *effects* that such ideas may have on the lives of people of color that matter, as these modern versions serve to prevent proactive programs of racial redress. The ideas associated with modern racism have to be understood as the indirect barriers used to stop the programs many feel are necessary for racial equality to be achieved, and are the indirect means to maintain racial stratification and the justifications offered for racial disparities.

A desire to find ways to overcome racism is not limited to the United States. In the 1960s the Convention on the Elimination of All

Forms of Racial Discrimination was adopted in the United Nations. This convention built on a human rights approach with its attempt to prevent and prohibit racial abuse and to monitor and resolve racial disputes. Learning how to deal with racial disputes is a global concern, and if the solutions we discuss in future chapters resonate in the United States, which is not even a signatory to the convention, then perhaps they will also be effective in addressing racial alienation elsewhere.

Modern Racial Conflict

To address the problem of finding common ground among Americans on racial issues, we have to comprehend the contemporary conflict in the United States. The old arguments of white supremacy are dead. New arguments concern whether we have achieved equality, what type of equality is sought (opportunity and/or outcome), whether institutional discrimination exists, and how to move forward. In the next two chapters, we explore previously proposed solutions and their limitations. Once we have studied these potential solutions we will be in a better position to offer possible new answers to the racial problems plaguing the United States.

THREE

CONFRONTING RACISM—MOVING
BEYOND THE PAST

Proposed solutions to racial alienation are not in short supply. Before we dare add another proposal we must examine already suggested solutions. Once we have gained an understanding of the racial solutions, we will then be in a position to situate our own ideas.

We categorize the proposed solutions by a criterion that helps us better understand the similarities and differences of proposed remedies. For example, the solutions vary as regards which racial groups are considered to have the greatest responsibility for implementing change. In some solutions people of color are expected to do most of the work to eliminate racial alienation; in other solutions majority-group members have the most responsibility for rectifying racial problems. This difference is vitally important, because assignment of obligations is connected to two distinct sets of presuppositions about our current racial reality. Therefore, we use as a criterion to situate the different solutions whether majority- or minority-group members are perceived as having the greater obligation for correcting racial alienation in the United States.

In this chapter we first discuss the organization of the general model by which we evaluate previous proposed solutions to racial alienation, and seek to explain the various solutions found within the model. However, there are too many solutions for us to present in a single chapter. Thus, in the balance of this chapter we examine only those solutions that are based on the obligations of racial minorities. In the next chapter we tackle solutions based upon the obligations of major-ity-group members.

Majority-Group Obligations versus Minority-Group Obligations

In analyzing proposed solutions, we found a tendency to put most if not all of the responsibility on either whites or nonwhites. In fact, it is fair to state that some solutions consider the entire burden of solving racial problems to belong to whites, whereas other solutions consider this burden to belong completely to people of color. Still other solu-tions consider both whites and people of color to have obligations, yet even these proposals place disproportionate obligations on either whites or people of color.

Given this tendency to apportion responsibility, we now have a basis for comparing the solutions with one other. Who is obligated to do the lion's share of the work is a critical to how solutions to racial alienation are advanced. Solutions based on moving beyond our past are linked to quite different assumptions than are solutions based upon racial justice. These different assumptions provide for a critical varia-tion in the worldview of those who conceptualize solutions that rely

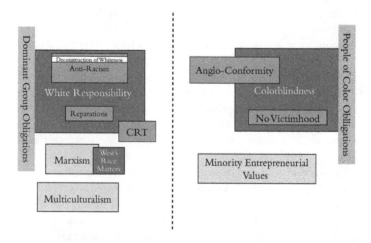

Figure 3.1: Model of Potential Solutions to Racial Problems in U.S.

on majority-group obligations and those who conceptualize solutions that rely on minority-group obligations.

To aid us in illustrating and introducing these various solutions in the context of majority- and minority-group obligations, we have constructed the model in Figure 3–1. The model can be understood as a continuum, with racial solutions based on majority-group obligations being closer to the left border of the model, whereas those based on minority-group obligations are closer to the right border. The sizes of the boxes are not important in the model; the boxes are sized to contain the description of the model. It also is not important whether the boxes are in the upper or lower portion of the graph. However, the solutions are not necessarily mutually exclusive. At times, some of the boxes are completely enclosed in another box (i.e., the Reparations box is within the White Responsibility box). This indicates that some of the ideas we examined are subsets of a larger philosophy guiding that approach. These subsets can be seen as ideological variations within the general framework of the larger solution encompassing that subset. As we examine each solution in the model, these descriptions will become clearer.

Whether the boxes overlap is noteworthy, because such overlapping indicates that important aspects of the solutions themselves have major elements in common. Thus, we claim, for example, that Anglo-Conformity contains elements of Colorblindness in that both downplay the importance of white racism, but these solutions are also distinct in key ways; notably, Anglo-Conformity recognizes certain cultural racial differences that may be missed by advocates of Colorblindness.

We should be reminded of the sociological founding father Max Weber's concept of ideal types. The ideal type allows the researcher to illustrate a concept with an exaggerated description that emphasizes the key characteristics of that concept. Weber argues that such exaggeration is useful for helping illustrate the various nuances between theories.

It is risky to limit the perspectives of scholars and/or activists into only one of the models we present. At times, an individual's thinking will fit into a single model. But it is also quite common that an individual is able to adopt the ideas of more than one model. The primary basis of the models is the group perceived as obligated to eliminate racial alienation. In this sense the question becomes: who is responsible for our racial problems—majority or minority group members. Those who perceive majority-group members' obligation as paramount tend to accept more than one of the models based upon that obligation as possible solutions. If not outright advocates for more than one model, they are at least open to accepting the goals of more than one model based on majority-group obligations. They place the ultimate responsibility for racial alienation on majority group members. The same can be said for those who base their understanding of racial issues on minority-group obligations, only that they ultimately place the ultimate responsibility for racial alienation on minority group members. Therefore, many of the scholars and activists that we will cite in this and the next chapter support more than a single model in Figure 3.1, but even when they support multiple models they see the same culprits—either majority or minority group members—as the source of our racial problems.

Our model provides a visual representation of the relations between ideas, thereby allowing us to assess how closely (or distantly) ideas are related to each other and to tie together complementary philosophies. Even though we have put all the ideas into a single global model, some of them are diametrically opposed to one another. The adherents of some of these philosophies would undoubtedly oppose adherents of some of the other philosophies on almost all racial issues. In fact, we argue that in many ways the advocates of the philosophies on the left side of the models rarely work, or perhaps even communicate, with the advocates of the philosophies on the right side of the model. It is almost as if these people live in different social worlds. Consequently, these people often have little knowledge of ideas on the other side of the spectrum and do not take these ideas into account.

Perhaps an illustration will help show the results of this division of social worlds. Imagine being on a steep hill. If a person goes down the right side of the hill, then it becomes difficult to see what is on the left side of the hill. Likewise, if one goes down the left side of the hill, then it is hard to see what is on the right side of the hill. Under these circumstances it becomes difficult to remember the other side of the hill. In this way those who head down the hill toward ideas that place the obligations of solving racial problems on majority-group members have a hard time seeing, much less respecting, solutions that are based on the obligations of minority-group members. The reverse is true for those who head down the hill toward solutions based on the actions of minority-group members. Furthermore, if the hill is pointed and narrow at the top then it becomes hard to stay in a position from which one can see and appreciate both the solutions based on majority-group obligations and those based on minority-group obligations. Thus, we have a natural tendency to head one way or the other and find ourselves in a social environment that replicates support for solutions seen on one side of the model and denigrates solutions from the other side.

We wanted to take special note of this division because it is vital to our understanding of conflict over solutions to racial injustice. As individuals head toward one side of the model, they become immersed in social and political subcultures that remove thoughts of alternative ways of dealing with racial injustice. The result is often alienation between the camps. This alienation makes it difficult for individuals on either side of the model to consider the potential value of solutions offered by those on the other side. We end up with a lack of synergy between racial solutions. Incredibly, instead of having intellectuals and activists of different political and social persuasions working together to solve the multidimensional problems of racial alienation, we have proposals to end such alienation that generate even *more racial and social conflict*.

A dotted line running down the middle of the model points out this division. The line is dotted to show it is not the case that the ideas are formally segregated from each other. The dotted line does, however, indicate that the advocates of these models rarely communicate with each other and rarely work together. Indeed, the holders of these philosophies typically occupy different social positions in the United States. The ideas on the left side of the model are more likely to be found in academic and leftist political organizations, whereas the ideas on the right are more likely to be found on conservative talk shows and right-wing think tanks. These different social locations lead advocates to have different social networks, which inhibits their exposure to the development of ideas from the other side of the model.

Solutions Based on Minority-Group Obligations

Solutions based on minority-group obligations ultimately conclude it is people of color who must change. These solutions attempt to challenge people of color to find success from their own resources, instead of relying on the resources of dominant-group members. These solutions also share a tendency to deemphasize the effects of historical and contemporary racism upon people of color. Such solutions remove from the majority group the responsibility of correcting the effects of historical racism. To this end, these solutions generally support the social and racial status quo in the United States. Therefore, it is not surprising that most of the supporters of these types of solutions tend to be majority-group members who benefit from the racial status quo.

Colorblindness

We start with colorblindness—that is, advocating seeing people as individuals (regardless of their race), rather than seeing racial groups, and assuming racial discrimination is, at best, a weak factor in limiting people's opportunities. We do because this proposed solution is the basis for most of the solutions that rely on notions of minority-group obligations. While one solution—minority entrepreneurial values—does not directly rely upon the ideas of colorblindness, all other proposed minority-obligation solutions have a strong colorblindness component. Gaining a solid understanding of this philosophy, then, is vital.

The seeds of a philosophy of colorblindness were planted in the development of the modern civil rights movement in the 1960s and 1970s. Before that movement, relatively few majority-group members advocated taking a colorblind approach to race relations. Those that did were more likely to have a progressive ideology as this colorblindness was used to combat the prevalence of white supremacy. Thus, many in the civil rights movement pushed for a society in which race would not affect a person's life chances.[1] Since the prevailing social order saw people of color overtly placed at a distinct disadvantage compared to whites, the idea of ignoring the racial differences had a powerful appeal for white progressives and people of color. This idea allowed some to interpret the civil rights organizations that developed in the 1960s and 1970s as institutions advocating removal of all racial differences in our society.

Because of this interpretation, some of the contemporary advocates for colorblindness (e.g., Bennett 1994, Horowitz 2002) were also involved in the modern civil rights movement. Such people were at least somewhat aware of the racism that those of color suffered, and saw the civil rights movement as offering a way to eliminate the disadvantages racial minorities experienced. For some of these advocates, the development of programs that recognized the historical effects of racial differences was a betrayal of what they believed they had fought for. They had fought for the elimination of the consideration of race in access to material and social resources, yet now they were seeing a movement advocating taking race into consideration as part of the solution. This incompatibility within the thinking process of such people made them less trustful of the civil rights movement and led to their unwillingness to continue to advocate for people of color.

To describe this betrayal, some who proposed a colorblind solution coined a new term—reverse racism. The concept of reverse racism is used to argue that any effort to provide resources to others based on racial differences is wrong. This includes overt types of discrimination but also contemporary efforts to compensate people of color for past racism.[2] Each is seen as an example of racism that must be challenged. This is a key argument that advocates of colorblindness use against programs such as affirmative action, which they consider to be reverse racism, something they perceive as providing unfair advantages to people of color.[3] They argue that whites who may be equally or even better qualified than people of color are not given the same opportunities, and so themselves become victims of racism.[4] To fairly treat both whites and nonwhites, racial considerations must be removed from all decisions concerning the hiring of workers and the accepting of applicants into educational institutions.

It is here that the core of the idea of colorblindness—the belief that racial equality will be best achieved if we can ignore racial differences—can be understood. For advocates of colorblindness, acknowledging racial differences is the source of our racial difficulties. This acknowledgment was the source of racism in our past, and it is the source of our present racial conflict. This is why some of the individuals who participated in marches for racial equality in the 1960s and 1970s can also be some of the biggest opponents of civil rights organizations today. They perceive both Jim Crow legislation, which legally separated blacks from the rest of society, and affirmative action, which explicitly helps blacks and Hispanics, to be measures that perpetuate racism. Such advocates acknowledge the pervasive unequal racial condition in our society, even as they argue that in the post–civil rights era we have relative racial equality. For these persons, as long as we treat people differently because of their race, even if we are doing so with the best of intentions, we will have the problem of racial alienation. Becoming colorblind, they conclude, is the best way to deal with racial alienation and injustice.

For example, the political conservative Terry Eastland (1997) contends that affirmative action is based on the notion of racial preference. This racial preference is in fact a type of discrimination that many in the majority accurately perceive as unfair. Eastland argues that, as a result of this unfair preference, whites have developed resentment toward people of color, which results in a backlash against people of color. He postulates that programs such as affirmative action imply that people of color are inferior and that whites begin to use this implied inferiority in their judgments of nonwhites, putting us on the slippery slope back toward white-supremacist thinking. White's judgment of people of color becomes based on the perception that non-whites need an unfair boost just to have any chance of societal or educational success. The source of racial tension then becomes the unfairness of affirmative-action programs and the perceptions these programs create. These programs claim to address racism, yet such racism was greatly reduced by the civil rights legislation of the 1960s. According to Eastland and many others, only by ridding our society of these programs and embracing color-blindness can we produce an atmosphere conducive to better race relations.

It is here that we see another feature of these notions of color-blindness, which is the idea that racism matters little, or not at all, in our contemporary society. The proponents of colorblindness commonly argue that racism now is not powerful enough to sufficiently affect the lives of people of color (Chavez 1991, D'souza 1996, Horowitz 2002). These advocates assert that while overt racism may still exist, the programs that we use to address it are far more powerful than what is needed to eliminate the effects of racism. If it can be demonstrated or assumed that racism is minimal (found among perhaps just a few "bad apples" with prejudiced views) then we have little need to pay attention to racial identities. Colorblindness advocates state that in a world in which racism is no longer a major problem for people of color, getting to a place where we can ignore, and even transcend, racial differences can help produce less contentious race relations in the United States.

Though majority-group members make up most of the colorblind supporters, proponents of colorblindness are not limited to majority-group members. One of the most articulate and well-known supporters of the colorblind position is Ward Connerly (2000), an African American conservative activist. Connerly argues that acknowledgment of race merely continues to damage race relations in the United States as it reminds Americans of our racial divisions. To overcome the damage that has been done by racism, he argues, we must create a fair society that has no programs favoring one race over another, with public institutions colorblind in their approach to everyone they encounter. Connerly is not a man unaware of overt racism. In fact, he recounts the racial segregation that he experienced early in his life and the harm it has done. But he also argues that this segregation taught him not to allow himself to be limited by race and helped him develop a colorblind approach toward racial issues. Thus, Connerly has taken the lessons of the modern civil rights movement and converted them into a plea for colorblindness.

Connerly is not alone in being a person of color who holds to some of the tenets of colorblindness. Other people of color (Chavez 1991, D'souza 1996, Elder 2002, McWhorter 2006, Steele 1990, C. Thomas 1997, A. Williams 2003) have accepted some degree of philosophical colorblindness as a way to combat the racial hostility that remains in our society. Some of these advocates argue that the focus on racial issues harms communities of color and that colorblindness is a way to improve these communities (Chavez 1991, Elder 2002, McWhorter 2001). They make this assertion based on the idea that people of color may misuse charges of racism to avoid looking at problems within their own communities. Others are concerned that racial preferences stigmatize people of color, making it harder for them to gain the social respect their efforts deserve (Steele 1990, A. Williams 2003). They argue that as long as we have race-based programs, successful people of color will be looked upon as having been given, and thus having failed to earn, their success. Regardless of the reasons for their support, this support is quite valuable for majority-group supporters of a colorblind philosophy, since having advocates who are people of color helps shield white supporters from a general charge of racism or self-interest.

One result of these arguments has been the successful effort to reduce, or even eliminate, affirmative-action programs in the United States. Connerly has played a key role in the passage of legislation in California that eliminated racial preferences in the University of California system. His effort inspired a similar successful movement in the State of Washington. These attempts to eliminate affirmative action are a natural consequence of the advocacy of colorblindness. Affirmative-action programs represent much of what colorblind advocates dislike about modern efforts to deal with racism, and thus they have been important targets for them. To the degree that supporters of a colorblind philosophy are able to gain and maintain social power, we should expect more such efforts to eliminate affirmative-action programs.

However, it is a mistake to think that affirmative-action programs are the limit of the reach of colorblindness advocates. They also tend to oppose any social programs and mechanisms recognizing the importance of race, such as legislation meant to reduce hate crimes, English as a Second Language programs in schools, and multicultural programs in colleges and universities. Any program or legislation that is seen as providing an "unfair" advantage to people of color is fair game for such advocates. As it concerns a positive initiative from colorblindness

advocates, one only has to consider "racial privacy," recently advocated in California. The initiative supporting racial privacy, which was
on the ballot in 2004, would have prevented the state government
from keeping racial information on California's students or state em-
ployees.[5] Although this initiative was defeated, it does show that such
advocates truly wish to remove all considerations of race from our
society. It is the push for ignoring racial differences and for equal
treatment for all races that drives this potential solution.

This emphasis on the removal of racial considerations is the core of
the colorblindness philosophy, and some version of this emphasis can
be found in most of the other attempts to address racial hostility that are
based on minority-group obligations. While other solutions may not
have the same degree of focus on ignoring race as is documented here,
the general idea of moving beyond historical racism is still a powerful
component of solutions that are based on minority-group obligations.

In sum, the tenets of colorblindness are as follows:

1. Attention to racial designations is the key cause of racial
   hostility in our society.
2. The elimination of attention to racial differences is the key to
   better race relations. Racism, racialization, and racial discrimination are not significant problems for people of color
   today.
3. Resentment of race-based preference programs is a significant
   cause of the racial hostility in our society.

The first two tenets suggest that programs that are race-based are
largely to blame for our current racial problems and must be opposed.
Tenet 3 supports the idea that attempts to eliminate overt racism may
be well-meaning, but because theses attempts focus on racial issues,
they also contribute to racial problems in the United States. Having
established the tenets of this ideology, we are now free to examine
other solutions based upon minority-group obligations.

A Subset of Colorblindness—No Victimhood

An important subset of the colorblindness paradigm is an idea we call
"no victimhood." It is a subset of colorblindness because advocates of
this idea emphasize major tenets of colorblindness to develop their
own unique perspective on racial issues. In particular, the idea that
racism is not a big problem for people of color in the United States

becomes the basis for this approach. If racism is not a serious problem for people of color, then how is one to interpret the actions of civil rights activists? Individuals who have developed a "No Victimhood" perspective on race relations tend to interpret activists who agitate for a solution to a problem that does not exist as a key source of racial hostility in the United States.

For civil rights advocates, it would be bad enough if colorblindness activists were merely mistaken in their appraisal of the degree of racism in our society. Yet many individuals with a "No Victimhood" stance do not attribute such a benign motivation to these activists. For example, Elder (2002) argues that many contemporary leaders of civil rights organizations are "victicrats," by which he means that these individuals have a vested interest in keeping racial issues prominent in the discourse. Since they have gained their notoriety because of their willingness to confront societal racism, they will be able to keep that notoriety as long as they can document the continued existence of racism. Therefore, these people will set unrealistic goals that must be met before they will agree that we have racial equality; this enables them to claim that racial victimization exists whether it does or not, enabling them to maintain the power they get from their social positions. McWhorter (2001) criticizes leaders of color for their propensity to create issues of racism out of small incidents, which in turn engenders feelings of victimization among people of color. Armstrong Williams (2003) argues that many prominent civil rights leaders use their position to gain prestige and power instead of advocating for people of color. These individuals are not really concerned with racial justice, but rather in maintaining the image of people of color as victims.

One may ask what is to be gained from victimhood. Steele (1990, 1994) writes that victimization enables people of color to make material and social claims on majority-group members. In a society of competing claims by different interest groups, being labeled a victim allows some groups to legitimate their claims by citing a need for racial equality. Those who are seen as victims as the result of societal oppression are often able to rally material and social support for themselves with this victimhood (Horowitz 2002, A. Williams 2003). Yet Steele also argues that the gain that people of color experience is negligible and the costs of this victimization is the dehumanization that comes from a lifetime of thinking of oneself as a victim. Little is empowering about being seen as a victim, and having the status of "victim" may keep a racial community in a state of dependence and immaturity (Chavez 1991, Horowitz 2002, A. Williams 2003).

In short, from the "No Victimhood" perspective, the source of racial hostility is the unjustified claim of victimization by people of color, especially their leaders in the civil rights movement. The solution proposed by those who accept the "No Victimhood" approach to race relations is straightforward: people of color must stop using an image of victimization to gain social and material status. Such short-term gains come at the cost of an inability to develop a solid community that can meet the needs of its residents. Rather than focus on racism, real and imagined, people of color would be better off attempting to better themselves and their communities. No real role for majority-group members exists in such a framework since they have not fostered this notion of victimization upon people of color. Addressing victimization is a problem that people of color must take care of from within their own communities rather than look for help from majority-group members.

Anglo-Conformity

A large part of the justification of Anglo-conformity is based on propositions similar to those that comprise the ideology of colorblindness. However, unlike the "No Victimhood"perspective, this ideology is not a mere subset of colorblindness.

Anglo-conformity is a term that was first used by Steward and Mildred Cole (1954) and further developed by Milton Gordon (1964) as a way of describing the propensity of minority-group members to accept the majority-group culture. Gordon writes about the acceptance of the culture of Northern and Western European Americans as a normative structure to which other European Americans are pressured to conform. This process is part of the great "Americanization" project used to enable Southern and Eastern Europeans to eventually become part of the majority group. In this sense, Anglo-conformity represents the idea that the way to build unity in a society is to compel minority groups to join the majority group's culture. Likewise, we use this concept to illustrate the desire on the part of advocates of Anglo-conformity to influence people of color to adopt majority-group culture.

In an important way, Anglo-conformity relies on some of the tenets that buttress notions of colorblindness. The idea that racism is no longer a big problem in our society is one that is quite popular among those who advocate an Anglo-conformist perception of our society (Chavez 1991, McWhorter 2001). This is not to say that historical racism is not a problem for communities of color, but the way this historical racism manifests itself is generally along the lines of societal dysfunctions that have developed within these communities (McWhorter 2001, 2006; W. J. Wilson 1980). For Anglo-conformists, to the degree that Americans continue to focus on efforts to find contemporary racism, they engage in a misplaced effort to solve problems that are not very serious. Accordingly, only when we begin to look within communities of color for solutions to our racial animosity will we be able to determine the root of the racial alienation that troubles our society.

So what solution do proponents of Anglo-conformity tend to advocate? It is here that we can see some deviation from the general notions of colorblindness. Advocates of Anglo-conformity do not totally ignore racial differences, particularly as they concern cultural issues. For example, Linda Chavez (1991) postulates that cultural aspects within the Puerto Rican community are slowing the economic progress of that community. She argues that for Puerto Ricans to succeed in our society, they must make cultural changes that encourage the development of the two-parent households typical of the dominant middle class. Likewise, Mazhar Ali Awan (1997) contends that African Americans in the United States need to develop a strong work ethic that can instill personal responsibility in all family members if they are going to close the income gap between blacks and majority-group members. McWhorter (2006) finds that the problem is the poor preparation of many African American students beginning college. He argues for an increased effort to promote academic excellence as a way to address some of our racial inequalities. In all of these cases, we see Anglo-conformity advocating an adherence to the values and practices found within the dominant culture as the solution to social and economic racial inequality. This admiration of Western European culture is the cornerstone of Anglo-conformist thinking. The historian Arthur M. Schlesinger Jr. (1992), for example, has argued that efforts to promote diversity should not abandon the Western ideals of democracy and human rights. Thus, unlike pure colorblindness, the philosophy of Anglo-conformity does note racial differences, but it does so in order to compel compliance with the dominant-group culture.

Achieving economic equality through adherence to the dominant culture is the key tenet of Anglo-conformity. Advocates of this philosophy tend to conceptualize economic inequality as a source of racial hostility. To this end, some advocates have discussed the economic successes of previous minority ethnic or racial groups (such as Irish

Americans or Italian Americans), or even current minority racial groups (such as Asian Americans) as evidence that economic success is possible for people of color (Awan 1997, McWhorter 2006). These successes are seen as the beginning of the assimilation of former minority groups into the dominant group's culture, and perhaps even into the dominant group itself. Once this assimilation takes place then the principles of colorblindness will apply and little reason exists for racial intergroup hostility. The attention paid to racial differences the key way in which the Anglo-conformity perspective differs from those who advocate a colorblind society. In fact, Anglo-conformity can be conceptualized as a temporary state that we will experience until people of color obtain economic parity. Once people of color reach that parity then our society can rapidly progress towards colorblindness.

According to an Anglo-conformity perspective, most responsibility for dealing with racial alienation lies with the ability of people of color to adhere to the majority group culture and values. Because of this emphasis, it is rational to place this philosophy close to the edge of the minority group obligations side of the table. However, one could argue for an important role for majority group members to play as well. Majority-group members have an obligation to teach people of color about majority group culture and values. It is the desire to disseminate majority group culture that leads to efforts that emphasize the teaching of the English language (Baron 1990, Huddy & Sears 1990, McGroarty 1992) and of Western culture (Federici 1995, Zinn & Macedo 2004) in our educational curriculum. Thus, while it is clearly the case that the bulk of the responsibility lies with people of color, majority-group members have some responsibility to serve as mentors for racial minorities.

Minority Entrepreneurial Values

We close this review of solutions based upon minority-group obligations with an argument that is not highly based upon colorblindness. This argument is based on the hope of people of color developing entrepreneurial values. At first glance, this looks very similar to the ideas advocated by Anglo-conformity in that these types of entrepreneurial values may be linked to majority group culture. However, the main advocates of this solution are not attempting to ignore the reality created by racism. In fact, they are looking for a way to address racism. The literature in this area generally centers on African Americans, perhaps because evidence suggests African Americans have undergone a higher level of racial alienation than people of other races (Gallagher 2004a, Massey & Denton 1996, Ogbu 1978, Yancey 2003b). However, these principles can also be applied to members of other racial and ethnic groups.

The well-known William Julius Wilson's classic work (1980) sets the stage for this advocacy of entrepreneurial values. He argues that historical racism has created a society in which African Americans have been put at a great disadvantage. However, he argues that the overt racism that once dominated of our society has largely dissipated. But the effects of that historical discrimination have led to the racial inequality that still exists in the United States. Basically, he insists that the mechanisms of class inequality operate to hold down the African Americans who were historically relegated to the lower rungs of the economic ladder. Those people have fallen further behind as the biases of class continue to work against them. On the other hand, African Americans who have managed to make it into the middle class find opportunities that they have never known before. Wilson now argues that, as a result, class inequality, significantly more than racial discrimination, is the modern source of the problems in the African American communities.

One might say that Wilson has adopted some tenets of colorblindness. After all, he contends that African Americans today are not highly likely to be discriminated against because of their race. However, Wilson is not advocating that we ignore the effects of racial differences, as it is historical racism that has created these class disadvantages within African American communities. Thus, it is important to pay special attention to some of the dynamics creating racialized poverty in the United States. For example, in his later work, Wilson (1987) argues that some of the disadvantages that developed in African American culture are due to dysfunctions within the black family, and these dysfunctions have failed to inculcate the social values needed to ensure success. While he tends to dismiss the role of contemporary racism in creating racial inequality, he does argue that paying special attention to the way that historical racism has created these dysfunctions—and finding ways to overcome the effects of that historical racism—are essential to helping African Americans achieve economic success.

John Butler (2005) builds on Wilson's work through his argument for minority entrepreneurship. Throughout history, Butler writes, people of color have found entrepreneurship to be a valuable way for coping with racial oppression. One of the most common theoretical models that has been used to explain the economic success of minority businesspeople has been the "Theory of Middle-man Minorities." According to this theory, certain individuals in an oppressed group carve out an economic position between the racial elites and the minority underclass. In doing so, these individuals develop entrepreneurial values that enable them to experience significant economic success. If economic conditions are right, this success can grow within minority communities, helping members of those communities improve their social station. Butler argues that while certain racial groups wholeheartedly embrace this process, African Americans have failed to recognize the individuals supporting it. Thus, Butler develops the idea of the "truncated African American middlemen." This theory contends that subgroups of African Americans—especially entrepreneurs—have developed values similar to the ethnic middlemen cited in previous literature. These individuals are responsible for much of the previously ignored economic success that both historically and today are part of the African American community.

Unlike Wilson, Butler does not downplay the importance of contemporary racism in shaping the social reality of African Americans. However, like Wilson, he argues that much of the difficulty faced by African Americans can be lessened through economic success in the black communities. These entrepreneurs, he says, can meet many of the economic needs of the African American community. However, they are still too small in number to meet all of the economic needs. There is a need for more "middlemen" among African Americans to maximize success within the African American community. To this end, Butler argues that it is valuable to create avenues whereby African American (or Latino/a, Asian, or Native American) entrepreneurs can be developed. He writes that too much time has been spent on studying the black underclass, to the detriment of our understanding of black success. Learning about the black underclass is learning about those who have not succeeded, and thus we cannot learn how to create minority-group success through such research. Accordingly, he argues that shifting academic resources from the documentation of the black underclass to the study of how African Americans have become successful entrepreneurs is long overdue.

The notion of African American entrepreneurial values is one that does not completely fit with the other ideas at the right end of the box. This idea is not based on ignoring racial differences; rather, it recognizes that the norms in our society may not be the same for people of color as it is for dominant-group members. To this end, the argument about the unique conditions that can create economic success for people of color is not the same as advocating the more colorblind perspectives generally offered in the minority-obligation side of the overall model. However, at the core of their solution, the advocates of this perspective believe it is the responsibility of people of color to create success among themselves.

Summary of Minority-Obligation Solutions

Solutions that address racial alienation can be classified as (1) the obligations of people of color or (2) the obligations of dominant-group members. We spent this chapter looking at the former set of solutions. Generally, these solutions support the racial status quo. This is less the case with the ideas of minority-entrepreneur values, though it can be argued that supporting minority-group entrepreneurship also supports the basic economic structure of the United States. To the degree that this economic structure plays an important role in racial inequality in the United States, these types of solutions reinforce a racial status quo.

Anglo-conformist solutions can also be looked upon as changing the economic dynamics, in that these solutions may enable people of color to better compete in the economy. But ultimately, these solutions tend to reinforce the worth of majority-group values and the racial status quo. Clearly, the solutions of colorblindness and victimlessness reinforce the status quo, as they call upon people of color to ignore the manifestations of contemporary racism.

Generally, advocates of these solutions claim that if people of color learn to accept that racism is a thing of the past and recognize that they have the agency to succeed, then we will see less racial alienation in our society. Moving beyond our past is a theme found time and again within these solutions. This leads to the deemphasis on contemporary racism as a source of racial alienation. Such solutions tend to be endorsed by whites and political conservatives who wish to maintain the social status quo or who view the dominant way of life as good and open to all.

However, focusing on the obligations of people of color is only one of the two major ways in which racial solutions have been conceptualized. Much work has been done to examine how majority-group members have contributed to racial alienation in the United States. To this end, in the next chapter we look at such solutions.

FOUR

DEALING WITH RACISM—LOOKING FOR JUSTICE

It was not people of color who created and institutionalized slavery. It was not people of color who created and institutionalized Jim Crow segregation, redlining, residential segregation, unequal pay by race, and the like. So say the scholars who disagree with the solutions put forward in the previous chapter. For these scholars, it is whites who must dismantle the racialized society.

But since the majority group benefits from the racialized society, why would it be willing to work against its own racial advantage? From a utilitarian premise, no real reason exists for individuals in the majority group to want change in the racial status quo. They have a vested interest in concentrating upon the responsibilities of minority-group members to ignore the past and to become part of a contemporary "colorblind" society. This is why the solutions in the preceding chapter are so appealing to them.

Another persistent problem for those advocating majority-group obligations is that past racial discrimination was quite blatant and easy to see. It required little effort to convince individuals that people of color suffered from racial discrimination. Eventually, the documentation of oppressive treatment of people of color aided in the passage of civil and voting rights legislation aimed at eradicating such oppression. However, the overt instances of racial discrimination that advocates once used to justify the majority group's obligations are not nearly as plentiful today. Somehow, these advocates have to find legitimization for claims upon the majority group that is not based upon the witnessing of overt discrimination.

To overcome these issues, solutions concentrating upon the obligations of the majority group have tended to facilitate the concept of
"racial justice." It generally is not enough for advocates of these
remedies to merely talk about racial equality or overt racial discrimination. Such discussions easily lead to the philosophy of contemporary
equality of opportunity and then to ideas of colorblindness. This takes
us right back to solutions in which the minority group has all the
responsibility to effect change. Rather, the notion of racial justice,
which dictates that we do not limit ourselves to looking at our contemporary racial situation, must be employed. We also have to analyze
how society has gotten to this point. The racial past cannot be ignored.
Justice because of past racism, even if the individuals who perpetrated
historical racism are no longer around to pay for it, remains an important consideration. Advocates of racial solutions that emphasize
majority-group obligations appeal to racial justice as a holistic approach
for racial healing and thus a necessary component in solving the
problems of racial alienation.

Historical racism is not the only source of racial alienation for
advocates of majority-group obligation. Such advocates argue that
contemporary subtle and institutional racial forces are destructive to
efforts to overcome racial inequity. Even though people of color have
legal equality, there is evidence that they continue to suffer economically because of modern forms of racism (Bobo, Kluegel, and Smith
1997, Gaertner & Dovidio 1986, Kinder & Sanders 1981, Kluegel 1990,
Sniderman & Piazza 1993). If we focus only on overt and individua-
lized types of racial bigotry, we miss the subtle and institutionalized
ways that racism continues to victimize people of color. Intentional
efforts to overcome these "new" forms of racism are another important
part of the solutions advocated by those who focus upon majority-
group obligations.

Solutions Based on Majority-Group
Obligations

White Responsibility

As discussed in the previous chapter, colorblindness is the general basis
for most solutions built on people-of-color obligations. Likewise, the
concept of "white responsibility" is the basis for most of the solutions
rooted in dominant-group obligations. Although not all solutions that

focus on the dominant group rely on this ideology, it is clearly the most influential idea.

Much of the idea of dominant-group responsibility is a reaction to the notions of colorblindness. Advocates of dominant-group responsibility perceive colorblindness as a way to let majority-group members "off the hook." Notions of colorblindness seem to suggest that majority-group members no longer have any obligation to end racial inequality. However, advocates of white responsibility argue that focusing on colorblindness distorts our ability to perceive how majority-group members continue to discriminate against minority-group members or support social policies that unduly punish people of color (Bonilla-Silva 2003, Dyson 1996, Guinier & Torres 2003). Those who advocate colorblindness call attention to the racial progress we have made over the past few decades; however, it can be argued that this progress has not undone the centuries of racial abuse that people of color have suffered (Brooks 2004, Feagin 2000). Ignoring that damage blinds us to the need to use racial justice to create a fair society. To overcome the distortions promoted by advocates of colorblindness, supporters of the notion of white responsibility emphasize the racial problems and social order that the dominant group has created (Derrick Bell 1993; Bonilla-Silva 2001, 2003; Feagin & Vera 2000; Hacker 1995).

To avoid focusing only upon our current racial reality, advocates of white responsibility also focus upon our racial problems because of past racism. However, unlike advocates of the minority-entrepreneur model, these advocates do not conceptualize minority-group members as having the responsibility for developing economic solutions in response to this historical racism. Rather, racial justice demands that the racial group that created the effects of historical racism—the dominant group—and its institutions are responsible for correcting these effects. It is against the inability of advocates of the colorblindness perspective to appreciate the continuing effects of racism that some supporters of white responsibly launch their most cutting critiques (Carr 1997, Dyson 1996, Guinier & Torres 2003). Since the dominant group has enjoyed the benefits of historical racism, minority-group advocates reason that the dominant group should also be willing to make the sacrifices necessary to help people of color overcome the effects of this racism.

Advocates of white responsibility do not stop with merely an assessment of the enduring effects of historical racism. They also look for the ways in which racism affects people of color today (Bonilla-Silva 2003, Churchill 1998, Delgado & Stefancic 2000, Hacker 1995). In doing so, they not only connect the racism of the past to the contemporary difficulties faced by racial minorities, but also make an argument that it is important to have race-based solutions to address current racial alienation.

For example, the problem of racial profiling is well documented (Arab American Anti-Discrimination Committee 2003; Gibeaut 1999; D. Harris 1999, 2003; Knowles et al. 2001). Advocates of white responsibility argue that racial profiling will not disappear without mechanisms to document the race of suspects who may be unfairly victimized by authority figures (Editorial 2000, D. Harris 1999). Solutions cannot be "colorblind"; rather, solutions must take race into account to eliminate the lingering effects of historical racism and the contemporary manifestations of racism.

This realization leads to a key component of white responsibility that helps this perspective to link together many ideas about addressing racial alienation. Having disposed of the desirability of colorblindness, advocates of white responsibility no longer need to create obligations designed to affect members of all racial groups equally. In fact, given their desire for racial justice, their ideas about the lingering effects of historical racism, and their conviction that contemporary racism is still a problem, it makes sense that such advocates would create solutions based on aiding the racial groups that have been deprived at the expense of those that have benefited from societal and contemporary racism. It may be crudely conceptualized as follows: If your neighbors have stolen your television, you will want it back. They can agree that they will no longer steal from you, but before you feel that the situation has been rectified, you want your stolen property returned. Until you get your television back, there is a clear sense that you have not received justice. The neighbors, then, will have to "lose" the television set they stole from you to meet their obligation for justice.

From the viewpoint of those advocating white responsibility, dominant-group members have stolen a lot more than a television set from people of color. Over the past few centuries, they have the stolen land, lives, and property of people of color. They have stolen identities, self-respect, and social standing. On the surface, their giving back what they stole may give the impression that dominant-group members are losing something, but according to advocates of white responsibility they are merely "returning the TV that is not theirs" so that we can have racial justice.

The core idea of white responsibility, then, is that whites have to change contemporary social systems to achieve racial justice. Which specific changes are needed for full racial justice remains open for debate. So the diversity of thought among those who take white-responsibility positions is largely due to the struggle over which solution may best aid this pursuit of racial justice.

A Subset of White Responsibility—Antiracism

"Antiracism" is a philosophy that has recently emerged and is generating significant research and activism. Advocates of antiracism argue that colorblindness is a passive attempt to address a virulent racism that refuses to disappear. These advocates say it is critical to take a proactive approach to racial problems. Racism is something to be openly resisted by those who are serious about ending it. As a result of this emphasis, a strong applied component has developed in the antiracism philosophy. Most writing generated from this perspective centers on how the proponents of this ideology can engage in activities that distribute the ideas and principles of antiracism to a larger society (Derman-Sparks & Phillips 1997, Gallagher 2004b, Katz 2003, Kivel 2002).

Dominant-group members are the focus of the attention of anti-racists. Several proponents of antiracism have discussed the importance of teaching dominant-group members about the effects of historical racism and/or the need for racial justice (Aveling 2002, Gallagher 2004b, Kivel 2002, Wildman & Davis 2002, Wise 2002). Antiracism has also becomes a program by which dominant-group members are taught how they perpetuate societal racism. Even if such actions and attitudes are unintentional, these actions and attitudes help buttress the racial alienation that continues to damage us. The actions to be avoided range from those that are obviously harmful to people of color, such as racial jokes, to those that are not intentionally aimed at harming people of color but do so nonetheless, such as not supporting political programs that distinctly help racial minorities. Concentrating on helping dominant-group members become actively "antiracist" is how this perspective promotes racial justice and resolution of the problems connected to racial inequity.

Antiracists face a major barrier: how to convince dominant-group members to become antiracist. This is pretty tough, given that it is rarely in the economic and social interest of dominant-group members to make such changes. To this end, the antiracists' solution offers a strong applied component, in that some of the research involves learning how dominant-group members may be able to make the trip from being either "pro-racist" or uninterested in addressing racial issues to becoming antiracist (Clark & O'Donnell 1999, Derman-Sparks & Phillips 1997, Lipsitz 1995, O'Brien 2001). Compared to holders of most of the other perspectives, antiracism proponents are less interested in theoretical exploration and more concerned with concrete, practical ways to help recruit dominant-group members.

Advocates of antiracism envision little, if any, effort to recruit people of color. People of color are not the ones who have ignored the damaging effects of racism; they are fully aware of them. It is the dominant group that has to learn about the real effects of racism. This has led to a focus on how dominant-group members have constructed a racial ideology that works to perpetuate their societal advantages. Producing a critical analysis of this premise of whiteness is a major and important conceptual project for advocates of antiracism.

A Subset of Antiracism—Deconstruction
of Whiteness

According to some antiracism activists, white racial identity (or whiteness) is a major part of the racial problems in our society (Ignatiev 1997, Lipsitz 1995, Wise 2002). Because our social structures developed to meet the needs of the dominant group, this whiteness has evolved in ways that maintain the racial status quo. To this end, a significant subset of individuals within the antiracist movement has made the "deconstruction of whiteness" a major emphasis in their actions to end racism. This deconstruction is an attempt to show the damage that has been done to people of color through the perpetuation of whiteness, and encourages dominant-group members to overtly address many of the racial issues in the United States (Clark & O'Donnell 1999, Ignatiev & Garvey 1996, Lipsitz 1995, Wise 2005).

A well-known contribution from this perspective is the concept of white privilege. Peggy Macintosh (2002) is generally acknowledged as the originator of this term, which she uses to illustrate the "unrecognized and unearned advantages" of dominant-group members in the United States. Because dominant-group members do not easily see these advantages, they readily dismiss charges of unfairness from people of color.

Deconstructing whiteness does not end with merely acknowledging the continued effects of racism on people of color. Advocates of this philosophy insist that whites should critically view their own racial identity and the damage whiteness has done to our society and to whites personally. In fact, Noel Ignatiev has coined the term "Race Traitor" as a way to understand the critical attitudes that dominant-group members need to take toward unhealthy features of their own racial identity (Ignatiev 1997, Ignatiev & Garvey 1996).[1] A "Race Traitor" becomes a white person who renounces the unfair advantages gained by his/her racial status so that he/she can promote racial justice. Other writings focusing on white deconstruction highlight how certain dominant-group members have made a journey from apathy or hostility toward people of color to the adoption of a critical attitude toward the dominant group (Clark & O'Donnell 1999, O'Brien 2001, Wise 2002). This deconstruction is not merely an intellectual exercise; it is a call for action in which the dominant group destroys the corrupt racial system.

A Subset of White Responsibility—Reparations

The argument for paying reparations to certain racial minority groups is based on the reality that these racial groups have historically suffered greatly at the hands of majority-group members. This historical suffering is not limited to a contained period that has no real effect upon the lives of the people of those minority groups today. Rather, this suffering has helped create some of the social dysfunctions that people of color now experience (Brooks 2004, Churchill 1998, Human Rights Watch 2001, Salzberger & Turck 2004). Furthermore, many argue that the successes that majority-group members enjoy today are connected to the historical suffering of people of color (Moorehead 2002, Robinson 2000, Westley 2003). Majority-group members have been able to unjustly take some of the economic and social resources from people of color. The requirements of racial justice demand this be corrected.

The notion of reparations is founded on the argument that people of color today suffer because of the historical treatment of their ancestors. Reparations' moral basis is in the idea of the collective responsibility of whites for the benefits they gained at the expense of nonwhites (J. Thomas & Brunsma 2008). William Darity Jr. (2008) goes so far as to argue that reparations are deserved because of the problems created by Jim Crow, and thus some of today's blacks directly suffered from racial oppression and deserve compensation. Advocates of reparations have generally used African Americans as the test case, but the arguments they support can be used to justify reparations for other minority racial groups as well. However, the difficulty these advocates have in obtaining so much as an apology for racial atrocities such as slavery indicates the level of resistance toward even symbolic reparations (Ansell 2008).

What reparations may look like can vary, taking the form of lump-sum payments to individuals, a trust fund to which qualified minorities can apply for asset-building projects, vouchers to purchase assets, in-kind contributions, or the establishment of new institutions that serve eligible minorities (Ansell 2008, Darity Jr. & Frank 2003). But regardless of the form reparations take, advocates contend that racial justice is impossible until a proper recompense to people of color for all of the racial evil done to them has been paid (Brooks 2004, Westley 2003). It has even been argued that the United States should be brought before the United Nations' Convention on the Elimination of All Forms of Racial Discrimination so that proper reparations can be decided. However, since the United States has refused to sign on to this convention, such an outcome is unlikely.

Reparations and antiracism, with their emphasis on the deconstruction of whiteness, are philosophies firmly embedded within white responsibility. Each brings a different emphasis on a component within white responsibility, but these solutions focus entirely on the actions of majority-group members as a way to lessen the racial hostility in U.S. society. But, solutions based on dominant-group obligations need not be based upon just the obligations of the majority group. It is possible to fashion solutions that are based mostly on majority group obligations but still allow for some prominent role to be played by people of color. One such possible solution can be found in critical race theory.

Critical Race Theory

Critical race theory (CRT) emerged in the mid-1970s among legal scholars as they tried to make sense of how notions of racial justice could play out in the legal system (Delgado & Stefancic 2000). Theorists argued for a need to address more-subtle forms of racism. In examining this kind of racism, which threatened to go unnoticed, many of these scholars began discussing the need for narratives that illustrated this new type of racism. The use of stories and narratives to illuminate racial problems is a major contribution of CRT. For these scholars, it is essential that we intentionally examine the racialized aspects of our society rather than merely pretend that we now have racial equality. Without intentional efforts, it becomes easy for people of color, and their plights, to become invisible to the majority group (Ladson-Billings 2003, Tate 1996). Narratives help reveal the plight of people of color. According to CRT advocates, we have to be honest about the racial inequality that continues in our society, and to do that we will have to overcome the social fictions masking racial inequality.

Although CRT started in the legal sector in our society, it is clearly a philosophy that has influenced many other arenas in the United States. For example, Tate (1996) contends that the integration of students into our educational institutions is not enough to compel real institutional change. This integration can give the illusion of change, but racial inequality persists, even in integrated institutions.[2] For real change to occur, there must be a redistribution of power, and people of color must acquire the resources that majority-group members already have. Only in such a case will we see the structural alterations necessary for us to create real educational equality for all races.

The concept of "intersectionality," which has emerged within the confines of CRT (Crenshaw et al. 1995), links some of the similarities between racism and other types of oppressions, such as sexism. In both racism and sexism, socially constructed aspects (i.e., race and gender) have developed not because they are real, but because they were needed to buttress the claims of the dominant group. Some advocates of CRT argue that it is important to explore how we construct these ideas so that their use against marginalized social groups can be discredited. The construction of beneficial ideas and philosophies and the deconstruction of harmful ideas and philosophies are an important part of what CRT can bring to those who wish to address racial issues. It is in this process of construction and deconstruction that advocates of CRT draw attention to the racial problems they believe are often overlooked, and find the ability to challenge harmful ideologies that work against people of color.

CRT challenges the dominant culture's norms of colorblindness and individualism. Because it does this, majority-group members are called upon to alter their (commonly accepted) (white) racial identity. CRT asks European Americans to make a much greater adjustment in their notions of race than it does people of color. Furthermore, the source of the problems people of color face is often perceived as the manifestation of ideas that have arisen within white racial identity. For example, individualism is an important component of white racial identity and its manifestation allows majority group members to blame individual people of color for their economic and educational difficulties rather than looking at the influence of racialized social structures. In this way, CRT conceives the majority group as the source of problems that trouble people of color. This situates CRT squarely on side of dominant-group obligations and even the white-responsibility model.

However, people of color are not totally without responsibility. They can and should participate in the process of challenging the harmful social constructs that have been created by the dominant group. In fact, it is unreasonable to expect majority-group members to make the changes necessary to alter our current racial hierarchy unless and until people of color show dominant-group members the racial problems from which they still suffer.

Despite the prominence of the white-responsibility model among the solutions that focus on dominant-group obligations, some solutions on this side of the box can conceptually fall outside of the white-responsibility box. These solutions are based on the idea that the source of our racial tensions is situated in social facts that have worked to the advantage of the majority group, but they are also solutions providing an answer not based almost purely on majority-group actions. Multi-culturalism perceives our racial problems as attributable to the notions of ethnocentrism that lead us to disrespect other cultures. The powerful social position of majority-group members affords the dominant group the opportunity to impose its culture on all others. Marxism envisions racial problems as connected to a capitalist economy that has arisen to benefit the dominant group. In theory, both majority-and minority-group members must work to overcome cultural ethnocentrism and capitalism, even though the main beneficiaries of these social structures are majority-group members. Therefore, we choose not to put these solutions within the white-responsibility box. These unique answers need to be explored, and we will examine them as we look at multiculturalism.

Multiculturalism

Multiculturalism, or what has sometimes been called cultural plural-ism,[3] has become a common ideology on contemporary college campuses and has filtered into many other arenas in our society. Multiculturalism is an ideological system that emphasizes respect for different racial or ethnic cultural groups.

Much of the push for multiculturalism developed from concerns that people of color may assimilate into the dominant society (R. Lee

1992, Parekh 2000, Portes & Zhou 1994). Some scholars argue that if such assimilation occurs then the culture associated with people of color will be lost (Bash 1979, Hirschman 1983, Newman 1973). A historical example of the eradication of the culture of people of color is the forced assimilation of certain Native American tribes, which led to their cultures' all but disappearing (Eschbach 1995, Johnson 1993, Nagel & Snipp 1993). Thus, a multiculturalism approach is directly contrary to an Anglo-conformity approach.

The philosophy of multiculturalism has gained prominence among those who critique Eurocentrism and has generated a concerted effort to find the positive benefits of non-European cultures. Supporters of multiculturalism argue that finding and including the best of those cultures that have heretofore been belittled and marginalized by the dominant society will enrich our culture (Levine 1996). Such inclusion will help people of different races learn how to respect each other, and this respect will become the foundations of more-harmonious and more-beneficial race relations.

While educational institutions have used multiculturalism more than other societal institutions, the effect of this philosophy is not limited to education. For example, it has been argued that a multicultural approach can also be employed in criminal justice (Barak 1991, Davis & Erez 1998, Greene 1997, Tarver, Walker, & Wallace. 2002). Understanding how people from different cultures approach issues of deviance and crime can help prevent and combat crime. Such an approach can also help us determine when there are unreasonable cultural expectations on certain racial groups and identify possible structural abuses in our criminal justice system. Work from a multicultural perspective has also addressed issues such as counseling (W. Lee 1999, Ponterotto et al. 2001, Pope-Davis & Coleman 2000), and business (Elashmawi & Harris 1998, Poncini 2004, Schreiber & Lenson 2000) in addition to other aspects of our society. So, multiculturalism is not just an educational phenomenon but also a philosophy that can help produce cultural understanding in a variety of situations.

Advocates of multiculturalism maintain that it is not merely tolerating different cultures but also working for social justice and the righting of the wrongs that have been done by the majority-group culture (Anner 2004, Miner 2004). For these reasons, it makes sense to discuss multiculturalism as a solution based on majority-group obligations. In theory, the practice of multiculturalism, or the acceptance of other cultures, can be emphasized among all racial groups. Unlike solutions such as antiracism—in which just about all responsibilities lie with majority-group members—multiculturalism is a philosophy that makes demands on individuals regardless of their racial background. In short, all of us must learn how to become more accepting of other cultures. Yet it is primarily whites—those who have dominated the culture for a long time—who must do so.

Marxism

Given the reliance of Marxists on the idea that capitalism is the source of social problems, it is not surprising that those Marxists who examine racial issues perceive capitalism as the reason that we have racial turmoil. For such thinkers, ending capitalism is the easiest way to eliminate racial alienation.

According to Oliver Cox (2001), capitalism sets up a society driven by economic competition. This competition motivates those with power to fashion social structures that allow them to gain a disproportionate share of societal resources at the expense of those without power. For example, Cox argues that slavery emerges in a capitalist system because it provides cheap labor for landowners, allowing them to exploit a segment of society marked by the perceived racial differences established to justify this exploitation. Since capitalism is a powerful social force that pushes individuals to support social structures that deprive others of resources, Cox argues that there can be no solution to racial problems unless we rid ourselves of capitalism.

Carr (1997) builds on the work of Cox with his use of the Marxian concept of false consciousness. The idea of false consciousness is that capitalism will tend to promote the development of ideologies that blind the proletariat (the workers, the have-nots) to their real plight in life. These ideologies become useful for the bourgeoisie (the owners, the haves) in that they help keep the proletariat satisfied, even while the bourgeoisie is exploiting them. Carr argues that the notion of color-blindness is an example of such a false ideology in that it allows people of all races to perceive themselves as being equal, when in fact our racialized society continues to work to the disadvantage of people of color. If people of color can be fooled into thinking that racial problems have been solved, then they are much less likely to acknowledge the real sources of racial oppression. However, for capitalism to survive it needs a constant source of cheap labor, which people of color provide. Therefore, as long as we have capitalism we will need to create mechanisms that fool those who have been racially oppressed.

The continuation of capitalism means the continuation of false notions of colorblindness (or similar ideologies). Carr contends that racial justice depends on replacing the hierarchal system of capitalism with the egalitarian system of socialism.

It is attention to this notion of racial justice and viewing majority-group members (the haves) as the culprits that allows the Marxism solution to be placed on the left side of the box in table 3.1. Yet this Marxian explanation does not quite belong in the white-responsibility box because, at its core, Marxism places the brunt of the blame for the persistence of racism on capitalism, and thus whites and nonwhites alike are encouraged to resist this system.

A Subset of Neo-Marxists: West's Race Matters

Cornel West's *Race Matters* (2001) is a relatively short book exploring his ideas on how we might be able to tackle some racial issues plaguing the United States. West believes that focusing solely on social structure neglects the socio-psychological dysfunctions hampering the African American community. Specifically, West argues that nihilism—that is, a sense of hopelessness and meaninglessness[4]—is pervasive among African Americans. This nihilism robs African Americans of their sense of identity, meaning, and self-worth. Materialist solutions cannot by themselves eliminate this nihilism; instead, the culture that has helped create that nihilism must be challenged. West argues that solutions proposed by well-meaning liberals generally fall short because they do little to remedy nihilism.

It is here that West turns to some of the critiques offered by Marxism in an effort to envision a solution for this source of angst. He argues that African Americans are trapped in a market culture which, coupled with the fears that whites have of blacks that has the created anger and despair that are the source of African American nihilism. Therefore, African American leaders must resist the influence of a capitalist market society. Yet, West argues, these leaders have been co-opted by the market system, developing a desire for status that robs them of their righteous anger and the authority they need to challenge racial problems. Only by resisting this market culture can African Americans rise above the social-psychological forces of hopelessness that have become all too common in their community.

For West, a major barrier to success for African Americans is the capitalism that dominates our society. To be sure, it is a capitalism that has been designed by majority-group members for their own benefit. However, West does not place all responsibility on majority-group members. Rather, he argues that we must find a race-transcending leader who will work toward a coalition with other races so that we can confront the alienating aspects of the market economy. Ultimately, it is the market culture, and not the majority group, that is the ultimate enemy of African Americans and other nonwhites. Resistance to this market economy is essential and must be the focus of our efforts.

While the focal point of West's work is African Americans, it is fair to argue that many of his ideas apply to other people of color as well. Because of the responsibilities that West gives blacks, it is inappropriate to place his ideas within the white-responsibility box. West's discussion of the anger blacks may feel toward whites makes it inappropriate to place his teachings completely within the Marxism box either. However, his critique of the market culture clearly makes his ideas part of Marxism, and thus we have placed his ideas to indicate that they overlap with, but are not totally immersed in, the Marxism box.

Summary of Majority-Group Obligations
Solutions

Each solution put forth in this chapter challenges the interests of the majority group in one way or another. They do not all require that only the majority group participates in solving the problems of racial alienation in our society. Those who are in the white-responsibility box do. But all of these solutions rely on majority-group members' surrendering some of their societal advantages so that racial justice can be possible.

Although many of the solutions on the left side of the model are separate from each other, it is clear that many adherents of these solutions are able to hold many of the solutions at the same time. For example, we placed the work of Manning (2000) among those who favored Marxism. However, his work also sounded the themes of multiculturalism and CRT. The works featured in Becoming and *Unbecoming White* (1999), edited by Clark and O'Donnell, tend to focus on the deconstruction of whiteness, but many of the works' authors are educational professionals who support multiculturalism. In many other ways, the majority-group obligations solutions are connected to each other by a concern for racial justice. This connection makes it plausible for people to value several of these solutions simultaneously.

Conclusion

In the preceding two chapters, we have seen solutions that begin from two main starting points—either racial divisions remain because of people of color or they remain because of whites (or their systems). We suggest that both starting points are inadequate for understanding and addressing our racial estrangement. We do not believe that we have to be stuck in only these starting points. A new, and more balanced, starting point can produce resolutions to the racial strife that incorporate many of the strengths of solutions based on both minority- and majority-group obligations. But first we need to critically examine the shortcomings of these previous approaches in the hope that we will be in a better position to fashion a more comprehensive solution. To this end, in the next chapter we will offer our critique of these approaches.

FIVE

WHY WE HAVE FAILED

Many Americans, mostly but not exclusively white Americans, believe that when it comes to race relations, we have not failed. Television, radio, and blogging pundits preach it daily, and millions of Americans readily accept it as fact. Race, as an organizer of inequality and mistreatment, is over. Racial oppression, save for the attempts of a few crackpots, is gone. Race relations, only occasionally strained by some old-timers who will not let go, improve constantly. Slavery, the racial caste system, and the Jim Crow segregation of the South all appear to be gone, eliminated, destroyed. We have a black president, so, clearly, what we have now is a meritocracy.

If group inequalities are identified (e..g., that whites have about ten times the wealth of blacks and Hispanics) and must be explained, the following justifications are offered by those who believe we have not failed:

- *The legacy of historical racism.* We have had equality of opportunity only for a few decades. It takes time for equality in outcome to occur, but it will.
- *A victim mentality.* Minorities still think it is 1940 and fail to see the opportunities given to them. (That minorities continue to think of themselves as victims is often linked to the work of minority leaders. Minority leaders are thought to want other minorities to keep the victim perspective so these leaders can keep their jobs and nice incomes.)

- *A culture of poverty.* For example, minorities believe it is "white" to succeed in school, or fail to think long-term to save and invest. Instead, despite wide-open opportunities, many minorities simply live in an alternative culture that values machismo, violence, drugs, illegal activities, and extramarital sex, and even celebrates "baby mamas" and the fathering of many children with many women. The continuing result is poverty and high incarceration rates.
- *It's class, not race.* The United States has economic inequality, to be sure. That there may be differences in average wealth across racial groups is in fact caused by persistent class differences; race no longer has an effect.
- *Avoidance of the group comparison.* The United States is a land of individuals. Comparing groups is wrong-headed. Oprah Winfrey, capitalizing on equality of opportunity and realizing she can be whatever she wants to be, is a billionaire. We should focus on the successes and celebrate our open society, which makes them possible.

We can find other explanations as well, but these capture most of what is offered. Again, millions and millions of Americans subscribe to these views. There is some truth in each of them. It is true, for example, that some Americans live in "a culture of poverty" that is not at all conducive to educational and long-term economic success. It is true that the legacy of historical racism profoundly shapes the present. No matter what changes are made, it will take a long time to achieve something approaching group equality of outcome.[1] It is true that some minorities blame almost every life failure on "the man" and do not take personal responsibility (though it is also true that some whites do the same).

Conversely, we have millions and millions of Americans, mostly but not exclusively nonwhite Americans, who believe we have failed. Racial inequality is in our face, ever present. It grinds down individuals, families, and communities daily. Race relations, though showing some improvement, are severely strained. "The man" engages constantly in racial oppression. Indeed, the entire system—political, economic, cultural, educational—is rigged to give whites the advantage.

If group equalities or major progress are identified (e.g., that blacks and Hispanics of the same wealth levels attend college at rates equal to whites, or that Asians have an average family incomes as high as

whites), the following are offered by those who believe we continue
to fail:

- *Wrong comparisons.* Comparing groups who have the same
  wealth levels is wrong because it assumes that wealth levels
  are not the result of racial oppression and inequality. But they
  are. For example, for many Americans, a good part of their
  wealth is generated through the increase in their housing
  values. But minorities are far less likely to own homes
  (through an entire series of racially oppressive, unequal practices), and minority neighborhoods' housing values rise sub-
  stantially less than do majority neighborhoods' housing values.
  So it doesn't much matter if people of different racial groups
  with equal wealth have many similar outcomes. What is
  primary is that it is rare for nonwhites to have wealth equal
  to that of whites.
- *Appeasement.* To appease minorities and keep the unequal
  system in place, individuals among minorities are allowed to
  succeed, providing evidence of a fair system. But only a tiny
  percentage will ever be allowed to rise toward the top.
- *Continued inequality.* Even with college educations, minorities
  end up in less prestigious occupations and earn less money,
  because the system remains racialized.
- *Honorary status.* To maintain their privilege, whites allow for
  honorary whites who are given many of the privileges of
  majority-group status. These honorary whites (perhaps light-
  skinned Hispanics and some Asians) then become supportive
  of the racial status quo. Whites have always expanded the
  boundaries of who is white to keep their power.
- *The velvet glove.* In some ways, many of the above explanations
  are incorporated into the explanation offered by Mary Jackman in her 1994 book. In marriage, if one spouse is to have
  power over the other, it is far more efficient and smooth to do
  so in the name of love, to have the partner believe you truly
  care for and love them. It works the same in race relations.
  A group can exercise military might over another to maintain
  privilege, but that gets messy and complicated. Much better
  in maintaining privilege is to be nice to the other group, to
  have them think you care, to be paternalistic, to invite some
  in, to treat them with a velvet glove. So, in the name of
  maintaining power and privilege, concessions are made to

minorities. They feel better, those in power feel good about themselves, violence is avoided, and yet the system, which perpetuates racial inequality, remains intact. For example, unlike in the past, minorities are now free to live in whatever neighborhood they wish. But the system of racial segregation in neighborhoods is maintained through other practices, such as more-secretive racial steering, the freedom of whites to move from neighborhoods if minorities move in, economic inequality, and so on.

We can find other explanations as well, but these capture most of what is offered. Millions and millions of Americans subscribe to these views. There is truth in each of them. It is true, for example, that despite decades of fair-housing laws, nearly all white children grow up in majority-white neighborhoods, as they always have. It is true that minorities with college degrees earn less than whites with college degrees. It is true that many Asian groups, while always faced with the question of whether they are fully American, are called "model minorities" by whites and often live in neighborhoods with whites, attend school with their children, and may become honorary whites.

Our Perspective

As we have argued, then, millions of Americans subscribe to one of these two perspectives. That we have such a conflict in perspective is not itself the failure. After all, Americans disagree on almost everything. We would not call it a failure that huge percentages of Americans are Republicans, huge percentages are Democrats, and many others are neither.

Rather, the failure lies in the strong, clear fact that the views described in the above section are racialized. That is, whites (and some honorary whites) overwhelmingly subscribe to the view that racial oppression is of the past, race relations are good and improving, and we have full equality of opportunity. All we need, as discussed in chapter 3, is for most nonwhites to come to agree with most whites and live like most whites. Nonwhites, though, overwhelmingly subscribe to the view that the system is stacked against minorities. It has always been so, and continues to be the tragic reality.

To be sure, many exceptions to this pattern of whites and some honorary whites subscribing to the all-is-better view and minorities subscribing to the biased-system view exist. Some of those "exceptions" get paid quite well and gain fame by telling the other group, "You have got it right." The other group loves such people. To be sure, if those on each side were aware of the racialized nature of who subscribes to each perspective, they would not come to see the other side as having a valid perspective, as we might hope. Rather, repeated historical and contemporary examples suggest that each would see their side as composed of people who see the truth, and the other side as composed of people who are self-interested or misguided.[2]

But this again points to our failure. The argument is repeatedly racialized, whether we label it thusly or not. Interest groups are part of what makes the United States work, but when they are racialized we have failed. In such a case, we are not Americans with various interests. We are racialized Americans competing against each other in a contest that cannot be won. In such a scenario, we do not have common ground. In fact, the way race has been lived and framed, even if we had common ground, both sides would consider such common ground failure. These facts, then, lead to what we saw in chapters 3 and 4—the burden of responsibility for racial equality being assigned, by those proposing solutions, overwhelmingly to either majority or minority groups, but not both. As Wachtel (1999) notes, "Our dialogue—such as it has been—has been accusatory and linear: *Who is the cause of our problems? You are.*" (3). And, in Chapter 3, Wachtel notes, "Incredibly, instead of intellectuals and activists of different political and social persuasions working together to solve the multidimensional problems of racial alienation, proposals to end such alienation generate even *more racial and social conflict*" (48).

What a mess. Let us look at our American failure more closely, so that we may inform our attempt to move toward success.

The American Racial Psyche

This American failure is not simple. It is now engrained deep in our collective psyches. As Wachtel writes:

> [Racial groups in the United States] are partners in a complex and fateful dance. It is a dance that can boast little grace and brings little pleasure, but it is performed with such perverse and practiced regularity that it is, by now, almost impossible to say who leads and who follows. Mostly without awareness, we each issue the cues that lead our partners across the racial divide to perform their roles and in turn to transmit to us the

cues that again elicit ours. In reproducing the same *pas de deux* over and over, we are caught in a vicious circle of vast proportions. A crucial element in that circle is our very failure to recognize that it *is* a circle, that we are *all* implicated in perpetuating it (1999: 1).

And as Cornel West wrote in his influential book, *Race Matters*:

> The paradox of race in America is that our common destiny is more pronounced and imperiled precisely when our divisions are deeper. The Civil War and its legacy speak loudly here . . . . There is no escape from our interracial interdependence, yet enforced racial hierarchy dooms us as a nation to collective paranoia and hysteria—the unmaking of any democratic order. (1993:4)

Despite consistent claims to the contrary by many U.S. citizens, social and psychological research consistently shows that we cannot live in this country and not hold racial stereotypes. They simply are ever-present, overtly and subtly. They float in the air, seemingly impervious to contradictory evidence, shaping what we see and influencing our interpretations, typically along racial lines, of course. This is not a matter of bad individuals thinking incorrect thoughts. To look at the issue of stereotypes in such a manner is to completely miss the fact that what we are talking about here are collective facts. In other words, stereotypes are not invented by any single person. They are created and sustained by a collective, long, imposed history, and, as we shall see, the properties of a particular hierarchical structure. Nearly all of today's stereotypes were around long before any of us were born. We learned them, almost by osmosis (for those who attempt to do so, it is always difficult to pinpoint how exactly we learn these long-standing stereotypes, probably because they are everywhere). Then, nurtured in a racialized context, the stereotypes appear to be confirmed by, as social psychologists show us, the way we interpret events.

To illustrate, take the long-standing stereotype whites have that, compared to themselves, minorities are crime prone. Now take the fact that whites commit more white-collar crimes. The crime stereotype that whites (and many others) have breathed since they were very young conditions them to either:

(1) not know or not notice that whites commit, in terms of absolute percentages, more white-collar crime, or

(2) interpret this fact as irrelevant because they view white-collar crime as less severe (or even less real) than street and petty crime.

Even though white-collar criminals steal millions upon millions of dollars annually, ruining thousands of lives, and it is whites who steal the bulk of it and ruin those lives, the racial stereotypes remain unaltered. Minorities are to be feared and cannot be trusted, for it is minorities, the stereotype goes, who are more likely to be criminals and who do most of the stealing.

It goes further. Whites are more likely to drive drunk, and therefore more likely to be arrested and convicted of drunk driving (see Wachtel 1999: 11–12). Drunk driving kills far more people per year than, for instance, muggings. But, again, because of the persistent stereotype of criminals, whites tend to dismiss such evidence, or fail even to see it. And, certainly, they do not ask, "What is wrong with white people that they are drinking so much and then driving and killing people? Why are they so impulsive and uncontrolled?"

Every few years for the last few decades we have learned of a horrible shooting committed by students at a high school or university, leading to multiple deaths. The perpetrators of these crimes are nearly always white. Yet only when they are not white is the race of the perpetrators an issue, and it is made an issue by those wondering whether the killings reflect a problem with a race of people, or perhaps with immigrants. When the perpetrators are white, though, we do not hear such questions as "What is wrong with white people, what makes them so violent, so crime prone?" Of course not. There is no such stereotype, so most people interpret such deeds as the isolated acts of mentally troubled individuals.

These examples of the power of stereotypes point to the severe constraints they place on us, and the powerful role of history. Humans are often shaped by their past—their early childhood, for example—in ways that are difficult to explain, name, and change. Simply saying "Get over it" or "It is not happening now" doesn't work. And simply saying "Quit being prejudiced" or "Those folks are evil for interpreting the world in that way" is no more effective or reasonable. Because we all exist in the context of histories—our own, our families', our communities'—changing stereotypes is a complex task. When members of different racial groups interact, as Wachtel notes, "each party experiences what is transpiring in light of past *experiences* with that group, *ideas* about the group, *feelings* about the group, and the concrete events that result between them as a consequence" (1999: 138).

Both individually and collectively, then, interpretations of events are mediated not only by particular stereotypes but by the past, the need to protect self- and group-esteem, and the need to define and defend identity. And in an age of political correctness, people's fears of offending others and not knowing what is (in)appropriate, leading ultimately to avoidance strategies, defensiveness, hyper-sensitivity, anger, hurt, confusion, and anxiety further complicate the problem. This is the stuff of potential volatility (recall the opening of chapter 1 to see that volatility in action). Combined with the reality of inequality and division, we have the ingredients necessary for the predictable combustion of rage, prejudice, self-doubt, nihilism, and guilt.

As Sandra Wilson's book *Hurt People Hurt People* (2001) argues, when we are injured by others we tend to act injuriously toward others, even if we loath such behavior. A child constantly berated by his or her parents often grows up to constantly berate his or her own children, despite a clear knowledge of the horror of such behavior. But injuring others leads to guilt. To relieve that guilt, we get the famous two-thousand-year-old dictum of Tacitus, the Roman historian: "It is human nature to hate those we have injured" (quoted in Myers 1993: 386). Summarizing the findings of more-modern social-psychological research, Elliot Aronson concludes, "If we have done something cruel to a person or a group of people, we derogate that person or group in order to justify our cruelty. If we can convince ourselves that a group is unworthy, subhuman, stupid, or immoral, it helps us to keep from feeling immoral [when we treat them badly]" (1992: 312).

We Help Our Own

In the book *Divided by Faith* (2000: ch. 7), Emerson and Smith discuss the paradox of group loyalty, which, in brief, is that racial actors (be they individuals, groups, or organizations) focus primarily on their own needs and perspectives, precisely because people and groups are acting morally. That is, the paradox of group loyalty makes racial actors self-interested.

How is self-interest moral? This question was explored by Reinhold Niebuhr (1932) in his book *Moral Man and Immoral Society*.[3] For one thing, he wrote, direct contact with members of other groups is always less than with one's own group. People thus know the members of their own group and their needs more deeply, fully, and personally than the members and needs of other groups. Therefore, they attend to the needs of their own group first, precisely because they are moral and loving. How can they turn their backs on the needs of their own group in favor of another group? A parent helps his or her children before helping other children. Neighbors work for the good of their neighborhoods before working for the benefit of other neighborhoods. At the individual level selfishness is usually considered negative, but at the group level it is considered moral and just. Indeed, at the group level, it is not selfishness, but morality, service, sacrifice, and loyalty.

The problem with this pattern is that the inequality between groups is maintained. Members of groups with the most share it with others of their group. Members of groups with the least are busy trying to meet the needs of others in their group, which, because the group has less, are typically bigger needs. It is a nasty cycle, even though the people involved are themselves not acting maliciously.

We have an additional problem, according to Niebuhr. Because the members of any given group cannot understand and feel the needs of another group as completely and deeply as they can those of their own group, relying on love, compassion, and persuasion to overcome group divisions and inequalities is practically impossible. For this reason, relations between groups are always mainly political rather than ethical or moral. As Niebuhr says, "[These relationships] will always be determined by the proportion of power which each group possesses at least as much as by any rational and moral appraisal of the comparative needs and claims of each group."[4]

The facts just considered have considerable implications for the perpetuation of racial inequality and alienation. Let's consider a few of those implications:

1. In the United States there is racial inequality in access to valued resources (e.g., white Americans have about ten times the average wealth of black and Hispanic Americans).
2. Access to valued resources—such as jobs, prestige, wealth, and power—is gained in significant part through social ties.[5]
3. For reasons such as social categorization, comparison, stereotypes, history, and the paradox of in-group loyalty, people have a positive bias for their in-group and a negative bias for out-groups.
4. Relations between racial groups will therefore be strained.
5. Importantly, racial group relations are, most centrally, political contests. They are, at the heart, about self-interested power.

It is time now to turn to proposing a new solution to the American failure. As the great philosopher Rocky Balboa said in the movie *Rocky*

(2006), "The world ain't all sunshine and rainbows. It's a very mean and nasty place and...it will beat you to your knees and keep you there permanently if you let it. You, me, or nobody is gonna hit as hard as life. But it ain't about how hard ya hit. It's about how hard you can get hit and keep moving forward....That's how winning is done!" When it comes to race, the United States has stumbled and fallen down. But it can get up and keep moving forward.

PART II

A PATH FORWARD

✦

SIX

LISTENING TO EACH OTHER

It is a simple, but often overlooked fact: a solution to addressing racial issues *has* to be accepted by both majority- and minority-group members. Solutions that fail to achieve a sufficient level of support from all groups simply cannot be successfully implemented or sustained. With this reality in mind, we begin our exploration by considering social situations in which multiple racial interests must be included for solutions to be maintained. Multiracial organizations, in which members of different races are forced to address cross-racial differences, provide one such social situation.

We know that merely throwing individuals of different races into a common social setting does not automatically lead to a lessening of racial tensions. However, if the members of those racial groups have an incentive to learn how to address racial alienation, then such contact may provide vital lessons for our macro-level race relations. For this reason, we must assess multiracial social institutions that have addressed the interests of both majority-and minority-group members.

In this chapter we first look at the contact hypothesis to identify multiracial social institutions that allow us to learn how individuals of different races have confronted racial hostility and alienation. Then we look at research on these specific social institutions and what lessons we can glean from them. To be specific, these multiracial institutions hold promise for helping us construct a more holistic solution to racial division, inequality, and alienation.

The Promise of Interracial Contact

What happens when people of different racial groups come into contact in social situations? Given a few conditions, the contact hypothesis theorizes that interracial contact produces more-harmonious race relations (Allport 1958, Amir 1976, T. F. Pettigrew 1998). As we might expect, it does not do as much positively for race relations if people's contact is simply standing in line at a grocery store (though, surprisingly, even this type of contact can have a limited positive effect). Ideally, social contact would help promote knowledge that leads members of all races toward a more positive affect, attitudes, and lessens alienation. Research on interracial contact suggests that these effects are most likely to occur if the contact happens under certain conditions (Allport 1958, Barnard & Benn 1988, Stephan 1987, Yancey 1999).

These conditions require (1) nonsuperficial contact (i.e., not the supermarket-type contact), (2) contact that is cooperative instead of competitive, (3) contact that is not coerced, (4) contact supported by relevant authority figures, and (5) contact between social equals. Although there have been some studies finding that interracial contact has only limited positive effects (Cohen 1984, Hewstone 1986, Jackman & Crane 1986, St. John 1975), these are overwhelmed by the studies finding that interracial contact is related to increased positive racial attitudes (Dixon & Rosenbaum 2004, T. F. Pettigrew & Tropp 2000, Stein, Post, & Rinden 2000). Studies find that all groups benefit from interracial contact but that majority-group members benefit the most; that is, their racial attitudes change the most, and they change in the direction of holding views more similar to those of minority-group members (Ellison & Powers 1994, Yancey 2003b).[1]

While recent research has challenged whether all of these conditions are necessary for interracial contact to alter racial attitudes (Dixon & Rosenbaum 2004, T. F. Pettigrew & Tropp 2000), contact within these conditions seems to produce the most powerful effects on racial perspectives. Thus, interracial contact in social settings that promote voluntary, egalitarian, cooperative, intimate contact that is supported by authority have the most potential for generating positive interracial relationships. For example, Yancey (1999) has demonstrated that interracial contact in residential neighborhoods is less likely to promote attitudinal changes than is interracial contact in religious institutions.

He argues that this pattern results because interracial contact is more likely to meet the necessary conditions in religious institutions than in residential neighborhoods. Other researchers have provided evidence that interracial contact in religious institutions has a significant effect on racial attitudes (Emerson 2006, Irvine 1973, Parker 1968, Yancey 1999, 2001). Likewise, research has suggested that interracial contact within families (Rosenblatt, Karis, & Powell; Yancey 2007a), the military (Mkandelbaum 1952, Moskos & Butler 1996), and athletic teams (K. Brown et al. 2003, T. Brown et al. 2003, Miracle 1981) also generates powerful effects because these settings meet the necessary conditions for positive attitudinal changes.

To date, though, contact-hypothesis research has generally been limited to assessing the racial attitudes of majority- and minority-group members at a given point in time, and usually with some standard questionnaire. We want to go beyond merely looking at whether racial attitudes are altered by such contact. We suggest that these settings allow both majority- and minority-group members to address racial barriers in the United States in a more comprehensive manner than the solutions given in chapters 3 and 4. The solutions offered in those chapters generally concentrated upon either the majority or the minority group's obligations. Individuals who have cooperative, egalitarian, voluntary, intimate contact with those of other races have to develop a social setting whereby the interests of all racial groups involved can be addressed.

For this reason, we contend that we can gain tremendous insight by examining social settings that produce positive interracial contact. Understanding the results of interracial contact within these settings not only points to what is possible if productive interracial contact becomes widespread but provides clues as to the type of settings that must be created.

We will not limit our investigation to looking for changes in racial attitudes within such settings. It is just as important to explore the cultural and institutional mechanisms created within these settings. Doing so will indicate why some social institutions are able to promote positive interracial contact. For example, why do certain religious institutions become multiracial while others do not? Why are interracial marriages able to have a powerful effect on racial attitudes (Yancey 2007b), while interracial intimate friendships do not tend to have such an effect (Jackman & Crane 1986, Korgen 2002)? These sorts of questions help reveal how certain social settings promote a more holistic racial approach than do other settings.

Dynamics of Interracial Contact

We have reasons to believe that families, religious organizations, athletic teams, social networks, and military organizations are well suited to meeting the contact-hypothesis conditions. We will call these primary social institutions. Institutions that are not well suited to meeting the conditions of positive interracial contact—such as educational institutions, residential neighborhoods, and most workplaces—we will call secondary social institutions. While some research suggests that productive interracial contact can occur in secondary social institutions (Dixon & Rosenbaum 2004, T. F. Pettigrew & Tropp 2000), more-powerful results should be found in primary social institutions.

Research on primary social institutions shows us the strong potential of interracial contact. For example, research on athletic teams indicates that interracial contact tends to reduce the level of racial prejudice among team members (K. Brown et al. 2003, Miracle 1981). Work on racial attitudes in the military indicates that exposure to individuals of different races is correlated with less extreme racial attitudes among whites and blacks, which allows for more racial agreement between those groups (Moskos & Butler 1996). Research on interracial families (Root 2001, Rosenblatt et al. 1995) and multiracial places of worship (Emerson 2006, Marti 2005, Yancey 2003a) finds that both whites and nonwhites make cultural adjustments to reduce potential conflicts within the racially integrated atmosphere of those institutions. These preliminary studies allow us to speculate that interracial contact will have a noticeable effect upon the racial perspectives of Americans.

However, closer inspection of research on interracial contact reveals that the effects of interracial contact are not the same for whites and nonwhites. For example, Yancey's research (2007b) suggest that European Americans in both interracial families and multiracial religious congregations are likely to alter their racial attitudes because of their contact with people of color, developing progressive attitudes toward racial issues. Yancey identifies at least three reasons that majority-group members develop such attitudes. The first is that they are able to listen to the racial issues that family or church members of color discuss with them. Somehow, interracial families and multiracial churches become a safe haven, in which majority-group members can hear about racism without being overly defensive. Second, majority-group members in these institutions often lose some of their majority-group status. This loss allows them to more easily identify with people of color. Third, the majority-group members in interracial families and multiracial churches are likely to witness incidents of racism, which challenges their previous perceptions of a colorblind society. It becomes difficult to deny the reality of racism when one observes a spouse's or friend's encounter with it.

However, we have limited evidence that people of color alter their racial attitudes because of interracial contact. Previous empirical work has affirmed that people of color in institutions where conditions of productive interracial contact are met are unlikely to have racial attitudes that differ from people of color with little contact with majority-group members (Emerson 2006, Korgen 2002, Yancey 2001, 2007b). Yancey (2007b) speculates that people of color may not alter their racial attitudes since they have thought about issues of race and racism before their contact with the majority group. If this is correct then people of color do not necessarily learn about racial issues from majority-group members, whereas majority-group members are able to learn about racial issues from this contact. The potential for attitudinal adjustment due to interracial contact is much greater for majority-group members than it is for people of color.

However people of color, particularly Hispanics and African Americans, do appear to gain economic and social capital from their contact with European Americans. Research documents that people of color who are part of interracial families (Heaton & Albrecht 1996, Hwang, Saenz, & Aguirre 1995, Morning 2000, Tucker & Mitchell-Kernan 1990) or who attend multiracial congregations (Emerson 2006, Yancey 2007b) enjoy higher social economic standing and are better educated than other people of color. Yancey (2007b) notes that there may be some self-selection, given that perhaps it is the better-educated and wealthier people of color who are more likely to interracially marry or join multiracial congregations. But he also produces qualitative evidence finding that not all of this effect can be attributed to self-selection, which indicates that at least some of the reason for this success is incorporated within the dimensions of interracial contact.[2] It is plausible to argue that people of color may gain social capital from their interaction with majority-group members. This social capital can translate into concrete economic and educational gains for individuals of color.

Some may argue that interracial marriages and multiracial places of worship may generally attract more-educated and wealthier individuals. However, research has indicated that majority-group members who interracially marry (Qian 1999) or join multiracial churches (Yancey 2007b) are not more educated or wealthier than other majority-group members. Any social-capital effects emerging from interracial contact tend to be limited to people of color. This leaves the plausible explanation that just as people of color do not gain knowledge as a result of contact with majority-group members that changes their racial attitudes, majority-group members do not gain social capital from their contact with people of color. The effects of interracial contact are that majority-group members pick up racial knowledge from this contact while people of color pick up knowledge and contacts that help them gain educational and economic assets. In this way, it is clear that interracial contact has significant but differing effects for white and nonwhites.

These findings may be linked to the unique settings of interracial families and multiracial houses of worship. Thus, unusual aspects connected to dynamics within interracial families or religious settings may have helped create these results. Individuals who do not interracially marry or who do not attend religious service may be immune to these effects. However, we contend that while these settings are somewhat unique, the result of this research is quite generalizable to our changing society and may help us conceptualize potential new directions in our understanding of how racial relations may be shaped in the future.

There are several other social settings where productive interracial contact can develop. For example, while many individuals will not marry interracially or attend religious congregations that are racially mixed, most Americans do have contact with people of other races. Therefore, most Americans are able to befriend those of other races. Racially integrated social networks have also been found to be associated with some of the positive changes noted earlier (Yancey 2007b). Furthermore, while the research into other primary social institutions, such as athletic teams and the military, is too limited to confirm these findings in those groups, it is reasonable to assert that similar effects would be found within these institutions. If such findings are discovered, then we will learn of other possible avenues in which productive interracial contact can develop. These are effects not limited to individuals who are in interracial marriages and multiracial congregations, since productive interracial contact is available to almost everyone in the United States, save those who live in very highly racially segregated areas.[3]

If this type of internal contact is available to most individuals in our society, then it is reasonable to ask why we have not seen more of it. If we have seen this type of interracial contact, and it produces the above changes, why do we not see more-progressive attitudes among majority-group members or more social capital among people of color? The answer to these questions is twofold. First, there is reason to believe that we will see more of this contact in younger cohorts of Americans. Research suggests that younger individuals are more likely to marry outside their race (Tucker & Mitchell-Kernan 1990) and develop friendships with those of other races (Briggs 2003). If this trend keeps up, then the future for productive interracial contact is indeed bright. Second, this type of contact generally does not occur without effort. For example, many religious congregations may want to be more racially diverse, but such diversity will not occur and be sustained unless there is a substantial, planned effort by congregation members to create it (Emerson 2006, Yancey 2003a). Many individuals may be open to having friends of other races, yet racially diverse social networks seem unlikely to develop by accident. Deliberate efforts must be made to enable productive interracial contact.

Furthermore, the problem is more than benign neglect. Interracial contact brings with it certain fears from current activists, who feel such contact will only hinder movement toward racial equality or will wrongly change the status quo. Ignoring those fears merely perpetuates the social separation we have seen thus far. Therefore, it is important to take an honest look at these fears to see if they justify the racial status quo.

Fears Connected to Interracial Contact

Some people and organizations today have significant fears concerning the promotion of increased interracial contact. Not surprisingly, those who promote majority-obligation solutions have one fear, and those who promote minority-obligation solutions have a different fear. Productive interracial contact will naturally create an environment in which both groups have to make compromises even though both majority- and minority-group members will benefit from the contact. But the reality is that both whites and nonwhites must make compromises, and this reality means that proponents on both sides of the current model of solutions are concerned about increased interracial contact.

The concern of those who promote minority-obligation solutions involves the attention needed to promote productive interracial contact. As we will see later in this chapter, and in the remaining chapters, productive interracial contact does not happen by accident. It occurs because of a concerted effort by both majority- and minority-group members. The majority group, in particular, must make cultural accommodations that help alleviate the threat that minority-group members may perceive from potential majority-group power. Advocates of colorblindness argue that to pay attention to racial distinctions is to create the opportunity for more racial conflict (Connerly 2000, Eastland 1997). Those supporting Anglo-conformity argue that moving away from the majority-group culture disadvantages people of color (Chavez 1991, McWhorter 2006). For different reasons, these advocates of minority-obligation solutions tend to dismiss any special effort to create multiracial social environments.

On this issue, the claim of colorblindness may be more popular than the arguments for Anglo-conformity. In our earlier work on multiracial congregations (DeYoung et al. 2003), we noted that many majority-group Christians adhered to the idea of homogeneous church growth. Homogeneous church growth is a perspective which says that churches should focus on attracting just one racial or ethnic group, because doing so will lead to faster growth than trying to attract a broader variety of people. Pragmatically, advocates of this perspective argue that because the church leadership is able to concentrate on meeting the needs of only that particular racial or ethnic group, people will feel more valued and cared for. This provides a nonracist religious argument that it is best for people of different races to stay with their own group rather than make an extraordinary effort to bring those of various groups together.[4] Likewise, nonreligious majority-group members can justify making no effort to incorporate minority-group members into their social lives if they can show that racially homogeneous organizations are more efficient than multiracial organizations. Thus, they can adopt the colorblind perception against special efforts to create multiracial social environments.

But we do not condone the desire of majority-group members to avoid the concerns of minority-group members. Rather, we believe that the effort to incorporate minority-group members into their social lives encourages majority-group members to help create a social environment that promotes racial understanding. If majority-group members wish to understand, and to be understood by, minority-group members, then ignoring people of color will be counterproductive. Despite the benign intentions of many individuals who promote a colorblind agenda, racial alienation in the United States will not disappear by itself over time. Like any social barrier, it will require effort from both majority- and minority-group members. If majority-group members adopt a colorblind approach, they will not have done their duty to help rid the nation of this barrier.

Neither does Anglo-conformity offer us a solution to the promotion of positive contact. The attitude that only majority-group culture is valuable is naturally offensive to people of color and will not produce egalitarian and/or cooperative contact. For our society to gain the full benefits of interracial contact, majority-group members must adopt an attitude that embraces both teaching and learning when entering into relationships with people of color. As we observed in the previous section, there is much for majority-group members to learn from productive contact with minority-group members.

But the fears of interracial contact are not limited to majority-group members. Those who advocate for majority obligations also are unsure about the value of interracial contact. Their concerns arise from the notion that minority-group members might eventually assimilate into the majority group because of the effects of interracial contact (Bash 1979, Hirschman 1983, Levine 1996), an assimilation that might smother the culture and values of minority-group members. Perhaps even more importantly, assimilation might reduce the desire for racial justice that minority-group members have developed. As we observed in chapter 4, this ideal of racial justice is at the core of majority-obligation solutions. If interaction with majority-group members reduces or, worse, eliminates the desire for people of color to seek racial justice, then it is natural for proponents of racial justice to deemphasize the importance of interracial contact.

In addition to their general fear that racial justice might be neglected, proponents of multiculturalism have an additional concern about interracial contact. Multiculturalism highlights the value of cultural purity, especially for those in minority groups. Interaction with those in the majority potentially threatens that purity and the very cultural elements that have allowed people of color to survive. Therefore, even if interracial contact does not reduce the desire for racial justice among minority-group members, this contact still may not be encouraged since it still endangers the maintenance of minority-group cultures.

However, as we have seen, interracial contact has more power to alter the racial attitudes and perspectives of majority-group members than those of minority-group members. In fact, research on multiracial places of worship and interracial families indicates that minority-group members are unlikely to alter their racial perspectives because of interracial contact (Emerson 2006, Yancey 2001, 2007b) and even finds heightened racial identity when there is interracial contact (Emerson 2006). Therefore, it is unlikely that the desire for racial justice among people of color diminishes because of contact with majority-group members, as long as that contact occurs under the established conditions of the contact hypothesis. If anything, interracial contact helps majority-group members become more concerned about racial justice. Interracial contact is a benefit, and not a barrier, for those who pursue racial justice.

We do acknowledge that interracial contact is likely to alter the cultural norms of individuals of all races. Religious congregations that are multiracial tend to adopt cultural aspects from multiple racial groups (Yancey 2003a). In this respect, the cultural purity of immigrant or racial or ethnic congregations is not maintained if those congregations become racially mixed. In interracial families there are also opportunities for different cultural elements to come together (Dalmage 2000, Luke & Luke 1998, Yancey 2007b). If the maintenance of cultural purity is the highest priority for social activists, then multiracial primary social institutions are definitely a problem. However, how valued is cultural purity? We contend that the maintenance of different cultures is important but that it is not more important than addressing racial alienation in the United States. We will later propose a balanced approach to the importance of cultural maintenance with the need for a unifying culture to enable us to overcome this alienation.

A Future Vision of the United States

What do these findings mean for the future of U.S. race relations and racialization? If, as we have argued, we can foster more social settings facilitating productive interracial contact, then it is quite plausible that we will see real alterations in our current dysfunctional race relations. The alterations will rely not only on majority- or only on minority-group members; rather, these will be alterations affecting both groups. Through making these changes, we hope to go beyond the majority-obligation or minority-obligation solutions we have relied upon to date and instead hope to devise a solution that will fall in the middle of table 3.1, one apportioning responsibility between both whites and nonwhites but also rewarding both groups as well. This is the type of "mutual model" that is needed for us to move beyond the overt and the subtle racial hostilities still plaguing the United States.

Productive interracial contact changes the racial attitudes of majority-group members. These changes do not occur among people of color, likely because they have already been forced to confront racial issues before the contact. This suggests that productive interracial contact helps majority-group members gain a deeper understanding of racism, an understanding which is often necessary to ally with people of color to work for positive racial change. Without such understanding, many majority-group members lack a sufficient understanding of the social structures hampering attempts to address racism. Along with others, we envision a new society, in which majority-group members gain more insight into how racialized our society is, and work to change it.

This interracial contact helps majority-group members challenge the social institutions that perpetrate institutional racism. We have noted many instances of this happening in our previous research. In our examination of multiracial religious organizations, we noted a white clergy member who, from his interaction with congregants of color came to understand why African Americans do not trust police officers (Yancey 2007b). We have also documented interviews with white spouses in interracial marriages who have observed racial profiling firsthand or see the need for affirmative action because of limits on their children's opportunities (Yancey 2007a). Productive interracial contact is going to generate more-progressive racial attitudes among majority-group members, which will help people of color challenge the social structures that continue to unfairly punish them. With enough productive contact, our current political racial dynamic, which relies upon colorblindness and which has seen the defeat of affirmative-action measures, such as proposition 2 in Michigan, can be changed to overtly address our racialized social structures. Thus, our vision of a future of productive interracial contact is one in which majority-group members develop more-progressive racial attitudes, which lead to more fruitful challenges to institutional racism.

However, our vision of the new society does not stop there. We must envision what is happening with people of color because of this interracial contact. As we stipulated, people of color can gain social capital because of this contact, increasing the probability of economic and educational success. A future generated by productive interracial contact is one in which people of color will have access to increased capital to achieve educational and economic success. Such success will alleviate much of the racial hostility generated by economic disparity.

Models of majority-group obligations suggest that without racial justice the problems of our racialized society will continue unabated. The vision of this racial justice is conceptualized as a political victory. While we believe that such political victories will be a part of our future, we do not think that they are sufficient for overcoming our racialized society. We have deep colorblindness wounds that must be healed if we are going to move forward. For example, research has suggested that African Americans suffer from lower levels of self-efficacy than do members of other races (Hughes & Demo 1989). Self-efficacy is the ability one has to believe that he or she can succeed in society. The lack of it inhibits the ability of African Americans to experience economic and educational success, even beyond political realities.

Our "mutual approach" differs from majority-obligation solutions because we assert that people of color can gain social capital from their interaction with majority-group members. This reality entails that people of color accept some responsibility for gaining that social capital. Some may say that this is a "blame the victim" approach in which we are attributing the dysfunctions of our racialized society to people of color. This is inaccurate. We are asserting what is clear—majority-group members are better suited to succeed in our society (unjust as that is), and people of color can gain advantages from access to the influence, position, resources, and social networks that majority-groups members have. We are not looking at a patriarchal relationship; the conditions of productive interracial contact demand egalitarian relationships between peers and allies. A Marxian approach would stipulate that the capitalist system we dwell in is the cause of white supremacy, and the solution is a transition to a more socialist tradition. But it is unrealistic to hope for a complete economic overhaul before people of color can get relief from racial discrimination. Furthermore, there is insufficient support for such an economic transition to occur anytime soon.

In short, political struggles have to be augmented with a striving toward economic and educational success among people of color in contemporary society. Neither political activism nor the economic and educational successes of people of color will by themselves completely eliminate racial alienation, but we envision that they will have a powerful effect. Simply put, *productive interracial interaction will foster great socioeconomic mobility and help us more fully address racialization than would our merely concentrating either on the obligations of majority- or those of minority-group members*. This interaction can transform the social world of racial hostilities we see today into one in which majority- and minority-group members have a level of trust and respect missing in today's society.

We seek a future where the economic and educational advantages of majority-group members are negligible and there is a strong mutual understanding of racial issues. The world we envision is one in which there is little need for racial mistrust because of the material gains people of color have made and the understanding of racial issues that majority group members possess. Creating such a world is a tall order. We believe that the spread of productive interracial contact in interracial organizations can go far in filling this order.

How Productive Interracial Contact Can Be Sustained

Clearly, not everyone is going to be part of interracial families, attend multiracial houses of worship, or join an organization such as the military. So how can we move beyond the current racial status quo to a world where productive interracial contact is commonplace? Lessons for the potential of such changes can be found in the very organizations in which we have seen the benefits of this kind of contact.

For example, why are some religious congregations multiracial while others tend mostly to attract individuals of a given race? A key to answering this question lies in the unique social structures of multiracial congregations. Inevitably, multiracial congregations are able to attract people of different races in ways that single-race congregations cannot. While there are several mechanisms that these congregations rely upon to succeed, an important one is that such congregations see racial diversity as a means to a higher goal (Yancey 2003a), such as evangelism, community service, or even political activism. Striving toward such a goal appears to be quite important in helping these congregations become and stay multiracial.

Having a higher, nonracial goal does not mean that such congregations fail to intentionally take steps to diversify. In fact, our previous work with multiracial congregations has documented the various ways these houses of worship purposely try to attract individuals of different races (Christerson, Emerson, & Edwards 2005, Emerson 2006, Yancey 2003a). However, rarely do these churches make becoming multiracial their most important goal. Rather, productive interracial contact becomes an avenue by which the multiracial congregations can achieve higher goals. For example, while conducting our study of multiracial congregations, we observed a congregation that at first was composed of middle-class majority-group suburbanites who wanted to reach out to the homeless. To accomplish this larger goal, the majority-group members were forced to address the racial and cultural issues that the homeless population—composed of people from various racial backgrounds—brought with them. In this way, the church's path toward being multiracial was fueled by the larger goal of serving a racially diverse marginalized population.

We learn an important lesson here: the goal of racial integration is generally not enough to foster positive interracial contact; it must additionally help such contact become productive—that is, give it a purpose. Multiracial congregations can more easily envision this goal than the goal of integrated schools and neighborhoods since religious institutions are meant to provide meaning for its members. In fact, it is the core values of religious organizations that attract members. The organizations can therefore make demands on members of the congregation, regardless of their race. For example, a pastor, priest, rabbi, or imam can sanction an attendee, regardless of his or her race, for "sins." Likewise, there are clear common goals in the (multiracial) military, which also exhibits productive interracial contact. Moskos and Butler (1996) note that positive race relations are not the military's ultimate goal but rather a means to the ultimate goal of combat readiness. Perhaps this cultural core allows individuals of different races to work together in the military despite the differences in racial perceptions and cultures that they may bring with them. Sharing an ideological core is quite important for shaping productive interracial contact.[5]

Clearly, a shared ideological core—beliefs about why we exist, or the purpose of society, for example—must be acceptable to members of multiple racial groups; such a core cannot be forced upon groups. In essence, it is important to ask what it means to be a member of this society. Which values are negotiable? Which are not? Which are binding on members of all racial groups, regardless of their cultures? This is not merely a desire that individuals of different races obey the laws of the country.[6] This core concerns whether there are cultural imperatives that guide us all (we explore this possibility in a later chapter).

We can be tempted to focus too much on establishing a cultural core, however. While essential, this core cannot completely engulf the members of all racial groups. For example, multiracial congregations generally accommodate cultural difference among members of other racial groups as long as they do not violate the core theological beliefs of the congregation. Multiracial families are not free to neglect the cultural demands of minority-group members. In fact, scholars have argued that it is vital for majority-group members in multiracial families to make accommodations for minority-group culture and values (Dalmage 2000, Killian 2001, McRoy & Zurcher 1983). Cultural freedom is a vital part of the success of multiracial social institutions.

This cultural freedom does not have to violate the value of having a common core. In fact, often this type of freedom complements the core. The analysis of Moskos and Butler (1996) indicates how this can happen in the Army, which they find does not compromise its essential values. Everyone in the Army, regardless of race, is expected to perform the required tasks of his or her job. However, on issues that are not vital to those values, the Army has shown surprising flexibility. People are allowed to express contrary racial ideals as long as those ideals do not challenge the Army's core goals. Having a core applied to all individuals can actually create the opportunity for cultural freedom. When we have a common set of values, then we also know what we do not have in common. Therefore, we can become free to operate on issues outside of the core culture as we, and our racial cultures, determine.

What we are proposing is *a revised understanding of multiculturalism*. Multiculturalism flounders in situations in which different racially based cultural groups are totally free to decide what is right for them. Such a multiculturalism leads to continued racial hostilities when these groups compete against each other. A healthier way to understand multiculturalism is as a philosophy that grants to groups the freedom to express themselves outside of a common core. In fact, we can envision this multiculturalism as the various expressions of the common values of our society, instead of as the expressions of each racial group's culture merely for its own sake.

To achieve this healthier way to understand multiculturalism, it is important to comprehend what that common cultural core might be in the United States. This is the difficult issue that often breeds, instead of reduces, conflict over which cultural values should dominate our society. This is why it is important to attempt to discover the values that are largely accepted by most racial groups in the United States. If the United States in fact has a culture distinct from that of other nations, then, ideally, the many racial groups that comprise our society will have picked up the same cultural values. In a later chapter, we explore research that will help us start to identify what some of those core values may be. However, clearly this will be only the beginning of a conversation we need to have about what it means to be a citizen of the United States.

Finding the core is only part of the solution. We must also change the racial mindset of our society. Successful multiracial institutions develop because the members of those institutions learn how to take into account the needs of both majority- and minority-group members. Think about how difficult a white—Hispanic marriage would be if the family sought to meet only the needs of the white spouse, or only the needs of the Hispanic spouse. Furthermore, few multiracial congregations can maintain their racial diversity if they do not include elements from the racial cultures of all members (Emerson 2006, Marti 2005, Yancey 2003a). Likewise, solutions to the problems of a racialized society cannot be addressed by concerning ourselves only with either majority- or minority-group obligations. The concerns of both groups must be taken into account for there to be success. The solutions postulated in chapters 3 and 4 ignore the obligations of either the majority-group members or the minority-group members. This is a key reason that none of these solutions have gained wide enough acceptance to drive permanent racial solutions.

Another lesson to be learned from these multiracial institutions is that all racial groups need to be heard if we are to fashion viable solutions to racialized issues. This means that it is important to find social settings in which both majority and minority groups can be heard and their statements taken seriously. There is great value in teaching groups how to take the concerns of other groups seriously. We don't tell a child to ignore the needs of her sibling. Why would we tell groups to ignore one another's needs? Teaching members of all racial groups that they are not free to demonize those they disagree with is similarly important. There is a long and overdue conversation about how we can solve our racial problems so that both majority- and minority-group members are satisfied. This conversation has occurred in some interracial families and multiracial churches. It is time to have a society-wide conversation, coupled with action.

Let's be honest. Racial groups have contrasting perspectives because holding on to those perspectives serves the members of those groups. This underpins group-interest theory (Bobo 2000, Tuch & Hughes 1996). White racial identity, in which we find the idea of colorblindness, supports majority-group interests (Bonilla-Silva 2003, Wildman & Davis 2002, Winddance 1997), and deconstructing white-ness is useful for people of color. Group interest, if harnessed and directed, can serve positive functions. So let's admit that group interest exists and is not going away anytime soon, and work from there (see the next chapter).

Our previous research has identified mechanisms that may help stimulate the type of conversations necessary for us to overcome racial strife. We found that multiracial congregations are able to provoke this conversation because they emphasize racially diverse leadership, make an intentional effort to communicate racial acceptance, and are flexible in adjusting to new cultural demands (Emerson 2006, Yancey 2003a). In fact, these tendencies are what help some religious congregations become racially diverse. This should also be true for healthy racial interaction outside of religious communities.

Furthermore, interracial couples have revealed in interviews that they negotiate cultural and racial issues from a perspective that respects those of both partners (Yancey 2007a). Even though the majority-group member tended to develop a more progressive racial ideology, the goal was to foster mutual respect not forced compliance. Childs (2005) argues that interracial romantic relationships still suffer from racial and gender power dynamics. But even with these dynamics, whites married to nonwhites are more likely to understand the plight of nonwhites than are whites married to other whites. So, elements of multiracial congregations and interracial marriages provide clues as to how nonreligious institutions can create an atmosphere whereby the perspectives of all racial groups can be respected. We explore this possibility in more depth in a later chapter.

Conclusion

Our society is racialized. What's the solution? Sometimes, the best way to find a macro-solution is to look at smaller-scale examples where a solution seems to be in the works. We looked at multiracial organiza-tions. Not all multiracial churches have handled racial issues in a healthy way, but those that have offer us insight into addressing racial conflict. Not all interracial marriages are successful, but many of them do provide paths toward creating a better racial future. The Army experiences racial conflict, but since the late 1970s it has done an impressive job of relieving racial tensions among soldiers and aggressively diversifying its' officer ranks. If we are going to find solutions acceptable to a significant number of people (of all races), multiracial primary social institutions provide important lessons, including:

1. Creating a common core—such as a shared goal—that unites those of different races.
2. Promoting multicultural freedom outside of this common core.
3. Fostering the development of true respect for all racial groups. (It doesn't work when one tells people what they must do, or enroll them in sensitivity training. It works when people see that, to reach a common goal, they benefit from respecting each other and working together.)

In the next three chapters, we explore applying these lessons to the nation as a whole.

SEVEN

Marriage counselors make nice livings—there is no shortage of customers. Marriages often falter due to selfishness, lack of communication, misunderstanding one another, and subsequently, mistrust and difficulty forgiving. Marriage counselors attempt to help couples overcome these problems by getting each spouse to see the other's perspective—put themselves in the other's shoes, listen to their spouse, and take positive steps to change the situation.

Racial groups are in a marriage, too. Their marriage is the shared society. Like the people that comprise them, racial groups are selfish. We call it "group interest." To move forward, the racial groups need "marriage" counseling. As in any marriage, one or the other partner will immediately react to such news with "I don't need marriage counseling, you do, because these problems are largely your doing!" It simply doesn't matter at such a point whose fault it is. What matters is that a marriage is in trouble, and all suffer from that trouble. The solution is to work together to fix it.

Listening to those of other racial groups is merely a start. How we listen is also important. We must consider taking the perspective of those in other racial and ethnic groups into account and not merely examining issues of conflict with a view toward how we can advance the concerns of our own group.

This perspective is not normal in human society. Theories of ethnocentrism (ethnocentrism is the belief that one's own group is centrally important and that all other groups are measured in relation to it) and social identity suggest that humans tend to protect the rights of their own in-group, even at the expense of other groups (Hogg & Abrams 1988, Sumner 1906, Taifel 1981). In the United States, this has resulted in our current racial atmosphere, in which it is expected that majority-group members ignore the racialized concerns of people of color while people of color denigrate the racial interest of majority-group members. The result of such processes is a society driven by racial conflict instead of by attempts to find racial consensus. Individuals quickly learn not to trust those of other races since there are no expectations that "honesty brokers," who do not merely support their own racial interest, will arise.

This chapter examines how the failure of whites and people of color to consider the interest of other racial groups has led to the solutions of majority- and minority-group obligations. To overcome the failings of past solutions, we have to find models where individuals and groups are willing to look beyond their own racial interests. The most obvious places to locate these models are in multiracial communities where individuals must develop primary relationships with each other and work together. Thus, once again, we examine research concerning multiracial families, integrated congregations, and the military. Doing so provides insight into the processes and rewards of developing an other-oriented racial perspective. A key reward is the development of interracial relationships that allow for honest cross-racial communication.

Ethnocentrism and Group Interest

William G. Sumner (1906), an early anthropologist, argued that ethnocentrism is a cultural universal. He maintained that such ethnocentrism is important for helping groups legitimate their norms and nonmaterial beliefs. This ethnocentrism also creates in-groups and out-groups. The out-groups provide convenient scapegoats for members of the in-group. This blame-shifting helps members of a culture maintain the belief that how their culture accomplishes its tasks is the best method, thus legitimating the social patterns of that culture.

Given this reality, it is not surprising that subcultures within a larger society also engage in ethnocentrism. They too have an interest in justifying their existence and method of accomplishing tasks. This often leads to the development of interest groups emerging to protect those subcultures. Advancing the work of Marx, Ralph Dahrendorf (1959) argues that interest groups consistently seek to gain a disproportionate share of social and economic resources, which they accomplish by max-imizing their power in society. They can then push for, or against, social changes promoting the interests of their groups. Accordingly, our social order is not based upon the most efficient way to develop a society, but rather on which group has the largest share of power at a given time. Interest groups do not support societal patterns because they are morally right, but because doing so serves their own interests.

Racial groups are clearly subcultures as described by Dahrendorf (1959); that is, these groups have certain interests that often can be realized only at the expense of those of other races. Consequently, they feel the need to legitimate their demands, and this process of legitimi-zation often becomes the source of racial conflict. Such groups may make claims based on concepts such as fairness, justice, equality, and colorblindness, but in reality these claims can be transitory. Their essential goal is the protection of their own group interest, and these concepts are useful only to the extent that they can accomplish this goal. Exploring how this can happen for majority- and minority-group members will illustrate how this process occurs in the United States.

Majority- and Minority-Group Examples of Ethnocentrism

According to the theory of ethnocentrism, actions of racial groups are tied to their attempt to gain resources in the United States. However, it is considered wrong and political suicide to support endeavors merely to advance one's own racial group. Thus, few if any advocates for the various racial groups in the United States overtly argue for racial policies advantageous to their own racial group. Rather, they imbed their arguments in larger concepts that provide legitimization for their concerns. Doing so allows them to make more global appeals to meet concerns tied to their own local interest. For instance, groups can call upon the larger moral concepts of fairness and equality of opportunity to legitimate an approach to racial issues that favors their own group.

For a concrete example, consider the mid-1990s case of Hopwood versus University of Texas. Cheryl J. Hopwood, a white woman, sued the university when she did not get into the University of Texas law school. Her rationale was that her LSAT score was higher than the score of several African American and Hispanic students who managed to get into the program. Up until that time the University of Texas was able to take into consideration multiple factors, including the racial background of students. It was an attempt to weigh the higher social, historical, and cultural barriers that students of color face. But for Cheryl Hopwood, such a consideration worked against her racial and personal interest. It was to her advantage for universities to ignore the effects of historical and institutional racism. She won the case, which removed the ability of Texas public institutions of higher education to use race in any way to consider admission to their programs. Her case outlawed educational affirmative-action programs in the State of Texas.

Advocates of majority-obligation solutions tend to be people of color and politically radical whites. The majority-group supporters of such solutions likely do so in keeping with an overarching political belief of progressive radicalism. However, people of color have a vested interest in the promotion of such solutions. These solutions focus on the need for majority-group members to surrender some of their social and economic power. Given their disadvantaged social and economic position, such an approach provides people of color access to resources they may otherwise be denied. To gain these resources, such individuals often look toward claims of social justice or equality. Our position is not that notions of social justice and equality are wrong, but rather that they are not substantiated purely by this larger moral concept. It is also the social interest of people of color that drives minority-group advocacy of solutions relying on majority-group obligations.

Sometimes the vested interest in finding fault in another racial group can lead to perversions of reality. A well-known example is the Tawana Brawley incident in New York City in 1987. Brawley accused several white men, including a police officer and an assistant district attorney, of rape and horrible physical abuse. Despite major discrepancies in Brawley's story and a lack of physical evidence, the African American community rallied behind her. It was civil rights activist Al Sharpton's role in Brawley's case that propelled him onto the national stage. The fact that accusations, such as those made against the men Brawley claimed had raped her, can easily destroy the lives of innocent whites did not seem to matter to these African Americans. It is easy to see why African Americans, despite the lack of evidence, latched onto this case, relying on a philosophy of white responsibility. Given the reality of racial discrimination, it is in the interest of African Americans to pursue any possible accusation of such discrimination. It is easy to see how people of color might use such accusations to protect themselves, even when they do so at the expense of majority-group members.

We do not wish to make judgments as to whether the Hopwood case or the Brawley incident is a more egregious case of self-interest. In both, certain racial actors advocate their own interest at the expense of racial out-groups. In both, there are unfortunate outcomes for race relations that must be taken into account. For example, few people of color are likely to accept that the Hopwood case was decided with their interests in mind. On the other hand, few whites accept that Sharpton and those who supported him were looking for a fair distribution of justice in the way Sharpton handled the Brawley incident. The outcome of these cases will never respected by all. Full legitimacy requires that all believe that a balanced approach toward racial issues was being practiced. Such legitimacy also depends on the perception that all sides have been heard and considered, something that whites in the Brawley situation and nonwhites in the Hopwood case are unlikely to think.

Multiracial Environments and Group Interest

George Mead (1934) developed the idea of "taking the role of the other" as a way to develop social relations. According to Mead, as we relate to others we generally attempt to interpret what they want through their verbal and nonverbal communication. When we appreciate what they are likely to desire, we can then decide whether to accommodate them. Notice that this requires that we make the effort to address others' needs. To some degree, bridging the racial divide in the United States also requires entering the mind of the other; that is, individuals must attempt to understand the perspectives of those different from themselves. However, ethnocentrism discourages us from making such efforts. To create a level of harmonious racial interaction, we have to recognize and confront ethnocentrism.

Research on multiracial environments provides insight into how we can minimize the ethnocentrism driving much of our racial conflict. One setting where we can explore that is the multiracial congregation. Because membership in religious organizations is voluntary, these communities must create an environment that allows them to attract and keep people of different racial groups. The philosophy of the groups' leaders provides insight into how such a situation is created.

A central component of this environment is the manner in which these leaders attempt to understand the perspectives of those of other races. For example, Yancey (2007b: 68–69) discusses a white pastor who came to learn how the African Americans in his church viewed the police. Because of his small stature and his race, he had previously perceived police officers only as a source of protection. Yet, many of his black parishioners saw the police as a problem for their community, a group to be feared. He did not automatically switch his perceptions to align with the view of his black church members, but his attempts to hear their concerns allowed him to gain a more balanced understanding. It also made him sensitive to the plight of his members of color. This new sensitivity undoubtedly enabled him to better lead a multiracial congregation, as he continually learned not to base his decisions purely upon the promotion of white racial interests.

This type of balance is not restricted to white religious leaders of multiracial congregations. One of the black head pastors of a multiracial congregation discussed why his church became multiracial, stating:

> We're very, very neutral in many of our ministry programs. My preaching is not any particular ethnic style of preaching. Our music, we try to make sure that it's not ethnically centered in any one direction. Those are things that kind of came naturally for us to realize, that if we were going to be a church that was going to be multiracial and multicultural, then we had to be diverse or somewhat neutral and so we made it easy for people of another culture to come in, to not have to contend with a lot of ethnic cultural stuff.

This pastor showed sensitivity toward creating an environment welcoming to other races. Pushing the church too far in the direction of a given racial or ethnic culture, he said, can serve to exclude other racial or ethnic cultures.

When this same pastor was asked what he did to make sure that his church remained racially diverse, he commented:

> To be a true, interracial, multicultural church, we felt that, of course, the staff had to be that way. The ministry head had to be diverse. The elders had to be of different backgrounds and we didn't do that for an outward show, but we prayed and God brought people of different nationalities that qualified as elders, so the staff, the elders, the pastoral staff, and the head of ministries.

Notice how this black pastor had to take care to include majority-group members in the leadership of the ministry. This was an intentional attempt to make sure that the perspectives of majority-group members were included in the church's decision-making.[1] Even though majority-group members have the dominant position in the larger society, they can be disempowered in a social community dominated by people of color. The black pastor of this particular congregation thought it important to make sure that this did not occur. A congregation that places an extremely high priority on being Afrocentric or Eurocentric or centered around any other race is not a congregation that can become racially diverse: such an environment is not perceived as welcoming to people from other racial groups (e.g., Emerson 2006, Marti 2005).

However, multiracial congregations are not the only places where we can learn about group interests. In interracial marriages individuals from a given racial group must address the concerns of those of other races. As previously discussed, several interracial families were interviewed about their experiences. In that work, one white mother in a black–white interracial marriage found herself defending a child of color from what she perceived as unfair treatment. She discussed this situation in our interview:

> My son kept coming home talking about the brown boy, the brown boy, the brown boy, and I was, like, who is the brown boy, and he said it's the new boy, he's the brown boy. And He said he's brown like daddy, you know, and grandma. Well, so I go to school and the little boy pushed [her son], and [her son] comes and tells the teacher. So I waited for her to correct [my son for calling him the brown boy], and it never happened. I said. don't you tell the kids not to call him the brown boy? She said, well, no, I didn't think it was a big deal. And, you know, right then I was just, like, the fact that you don't think it's a big deal bothers me because she, didn't have a clue.

The mother chose to look at the racial issues surrounding the the new boy and her son rather than address the fact that her child was pushed. She took into consideration the racial interests of the new boy and her child, which is not the same as her own racial interests, or even her own parental issue of her boy being pushed. Her experience being in a multiracial marriage undoubtedly made her more sensitive to potential racial issues in that school. Another white mother also showed such a concern when she remarked to us, during an interview, "The fact is that I'm raising what society considers a black male. I want him to have the same equal access to schools that a white kid has, and right now I think the only way that can be guaranteed is through affirmative action." These examples indicate that a white member in a multiracial family can take into consideration nonwhite racial interests.

Once again, it is not only white members of the family who must learn to consider others' concerns. In this research, members of interracial couples were asked questions about cultural differences in their marriages. While majority-group members were more likely to alter their racial attitudes as a result of interracial contact, white and non-white members were equally likely to make cultural adjustments for the marriage. For example, in the following excerpts from our interviews, we see two examples of spouses of color making adjustments by celebrating holidays they did not celebrate as children.

> It's, like, now I celebrate, St. Patrick's Day. I never even knew there was such a thing as St. Patrick's Day. I don't remember doing. New Year's or that kind of stuff. We didn't go into that sort of thing. It was just several things that we just didn't do, that we now do. (Hispanic woman married to a white man)

> I know that Thanksgiving and Christmas are big . . . so that's what we are doing, but I'm still trying because I know that there are some other holidays that were important to him when he was growing up, but I didn't celebrate. I learn for him. (Asian woman married to a white man)

Holidays were not the only cultural adjustment that these spouses of color made. Some of them also made adjustments in the type of music they listened to.

> She doesn't like hip-hop and mostly because some of the hip-hop that I listen to has profanity, and so she doesn't like that. So I don't listen to it with the kids, of course, and I don't listen to it around her 'cause she doesn't like (the profanity). But she is learning to like the music, the cleaner hip-hop songs. (Black man married to a white woman)

> I grew up with all different kinds of people, so I listen to all different kinds of music, but rarely rock-and-roll-type music. Now my wife has gotten me to listen to more rock-and-roll music, 'cause, you know, that's what she usually listens to . . . (Black man married to a white woman)

This last example indicates altered perspectives on higher education. A black woman married to a white man reflected:

> When I first married him, I'm thinking, okay, here's a guy that's a great guy, he's got a great education, you know, he'll want to roam the world—and that's so not him. He's just happy doing whatever. He just wants to be happy doing whatever he's doing, so I look at him and, I think, he has got this college education, he's extremely smart, he could be working in, you know, one of these Fortune 500 companies, but he's working doing something he loves, you know. And here I am, I don't have a college degree and I'm working for this big company making more money than my husband, and I guess my whole thing is, it's like, college and education is important, but it's not everything, even though

> I want it for my son just for him to have it. But then I think having that
> education allows some choices that I probably don't have.... So yeah,
> I think being married to him with a degree did affect how I felt about
> education.

In sum, we have evidence that people in interracial marriages, regardless of racial background, make cultural adjustments to maintain healthy, interracial marriages.

To create norms and values within a multiracial community, it is imperative that multiple racial interests be taken into account. Overcoming racial ethnocentrism is critical for creating and sustaining a multiracial environment. In the cases of multiracial congregations, the motivation for addressing ethnocentrism stems from a desire to grow and sustain a multiracial community of faith. For interracial families, the motivation for addressing ethnocentrism stems from a desire for a healthy, caring marriage and family life. Regardless of the source of the motivation for overcoming ethnocentrism, addressing group interest is a nonnegotiable.

Interracial Communication and Group Interest

Without trust—the belief that others care about more than their own needs—communication breaks down. The actions and attitudes demonstrated in the preceding section are examples of individuals who are "honesty brokers"; that is, people who can be trusted. They were willing to consider the concerns of racial out-groups, yet not give up their own concerns. Over time, these individuals gain legitimacy with people in other racial groups. Organizations, too, can become "honesty brokers," by considering and attempting to meet the concerns of multiple groups and by avoiding favoring one group over another.

Moskos and Butler (1996) argue that the U.S. Army has, over time, become an honesty broker. In their book, these scholars focus on the white/black racial divide and how the Army addresses that conflict. They contend that the Army must consider both the disadvantages that blacks have faced and the need that whites have to believe that blacks they work with, and for, have earned their positions. To accomplish this goal, the Army developed an approach to race relations that distinguished them from other social institutions. Moskos and Butler advocate a variety of lessons to be learned by the Army's method, including focusing on black opportunity, ruthlessly opposing discrimination, installing black leaders as soon as possible, linking affirmative action to standards, and enhancing black participation. These suggestions attempt to address the needs and concerns of those of both races, which one would expect in a social atmosphere wherein individuals of different races must interact with each other in primary relationships.

Organizations, such as educational institutions, where interracial relationships tend to be secondary, are free to concentrate on only solutions that focus on addressing the concerns of some racial groups. Given the progressive attitudes of many educators, there is little wonder that educational institutions tended to focus on solutions involving majority-group obligations such as multiculturalism and anti-racism. While these solutions meet real needs for people of color, they generally fail to attract sufficient support from majority-group members.

Chris Rice (2003), a white Christian, discusses a situation in his multiracial church, and in so doing illustrates the benefits of considering the interests of multiple racial groups in developing communication to resolve interracial conflict. He joined a black–white church in Mississippi. After serving in a leadership role in this ministry for a time, he saw interracial hostility begin to develop between the leaders who were white and the African Americans in the church. Evidently, many of the African Americans resented whites because they perceived that whites had taken over many of the leadership roles in the church. Instead of stewing, blowing up, or a mass exodus of people, the church held a series of "racial reconciliation" meetings wherein blacks vented their frustration. Rice decided to stay, even though he felt rejected. Changes were made. Over time, more African Americans gain more leadership roles in the church. However, Rice, too, maintained a leadership role, and eventually learned that the black members did not want to kick him out of the leadership; they wanted to share the leadership roles.

Both whites and blacks in the church soon realized that there was much work to do there and that there were many talented people to do the work. The best way to help the multiracial ministry succeed was to share the load. To this end, they created a leadership structure that consciously drew from both racial groups and focused on the needs of all in the congregation, rather than having a leadership structure of primarily one group. This arrangement eventually allowed Rice to join his co-ministry partner Spencer Perkins in writing a book discussing the lessons they learned from their experience (Perkins & Rice 2000).

Rice's story gives us special insight since it shows that Rice himself had to learn to look at the situation from the point of view of the African Americans, even as the African Americans had to learn to find a role for Rice. Honest communication had to develop to allow each party to comprehend the position of the other racial group. Multiracial communities find ways to address the concerns of several racial groups. If such accommodation and communication are to be sustainable, there must be not a defensive social atmosphere but a social atmosphere in which people of different races are free to be honest, yet respectful, with each other. We admit that, in some ways, this sounds trite ("Can't we all just get along?" as they said after the Los Angeles riots of the early 1990s), but there is no way around these truths. We have studied multiracial contexts for many years, and to be healthy and sustainable, they must always value open communication and respect.

Overcoming Group Interest

Every group protects its own group's interests. Thus, we should not quickly judge those who seem to promote only measures and activities that further the interests of their own racial group. They are doing what is natural. Overcoming racial-group interests, as is often done in interracial families and multiracial churches, is not the norm for most of us in most contexts. Therefore, we must ask how individuals in these multiracial contexts are able to "overcome nature" to walk in one another's shoes.

We might conceive of this phenomenon as adopting a "global interest" rather than a "tribal interest." To understand how it is possible to do so, we need to have goals larger than our own group's. In the next chapter, we look at how a core value system might help us heal societal schisms. But for now, we explore how racial unity itself is seen as a value by those in multiracial institutions and how this value allows the members of these institutions to consider others' interests.

For example, we logically assume that the members of a multiracial family value the racial diversity of the family. Since members of the family cannot alter their personal racial designation (at least, as race is defined in the United States), the only other real alternative to valuing that diversity is to dissolve the family. This reality creates a pressing need for the members of a multiracial family to find ways to accept racial diversity, and thus to look at the racial interests of others. Likewise, religious institutions are voluntary organizations that benefit

from attracting and keeping members. Consequently, multiracial religious organizations have a vested interest in looking after the concerns of multiple racial groups, rather than just one.[2]

Clearly, we can see why racial diversity is valued in and of itself in
multiracial institutions. Yet, such a value fails to provide sufficient
motivation for Americans to overcome all the barriers to racial whole-
ness. However, there is a vital place for the valuing of racial diversity.
If the members of a multiracial institution realize that racial diversity
will enable them to reach the group's goals (family cohesion or the
church's growth or mission), then it become much easier for the
members of that organization to work to understand the desires and
needs of those in other racial groups. In short, to the extent that valuing
racial diversity enables people to appreciate racial interests different
from their own, it is desirable, even if valuing racial diversity does not,
by itself, produce a multiracial community.

Conclusion

A multiracial community cannot be built to serve the interest of a
single racial group. For the community to survive and thrive, its
members must learn to consider the interests of members outside
their own racial group.[3]

If we want comprehensive solutions, we have to bring together
individuals who are willing to consider avenues that pay dividends not
only for one's own racial group. Multiracial groups of individuals who
value racial diversity more than they value their own group's interests
seem able to develop solutions to the racial issues that they confront or
that exist in the larger community. Sustainable multiracial communities have something in common—they value racial diversity, but
they also share a larger goal, a common set of beliefs or motivations for
existing, a larger purpose for which they strive. In the next chapter, we
will take a deeper look at the importance of such goals and the process
of developing them.

EIGHT

Multiculturalism is a philosophy emphasizing cultural maintenance. Our values are an essential part of our culture. Thus,
multiculturalism can lead to the promotion of multiple sets of values.
As we already noted, multiculturalism is a philosophy that has become
popular among some who advocate solutions based on majority-group
responsibility. Multiculturalism offers many valuable insights for the
eradication of racial tensions. It also is a philosophy that can inhibit the
development of value consensus because of the multiple sets of values
that can emerge. And developing value consensus is a must if racial
unity is to become a viable reality in the United States.

Earlier we discussed the need to develop a cultural core that can help
bond the various racial groups in the United States. While there has been
a great deal of academic discussion about the values that unite Americans,
there has been little empirical analysis documenting what Americans
believe those values are. In this chapter we use some preliminary research
to explore what our core values might look like. In doing so we take the
initial steps toward envisioning a set of values that can unify all Americans.
Of course, there is much work to be done before we can conceptualize a
complete version of such a core. The desires and interests of the various
racial groups have to be taken into consideration before we can fully
identify the common core. This chapter seeks to move us toward the
development of a common core, but it is not the last word.

To work toward outlining a common core, we use qualitative
research we conducted in our study of multiracial organizations,

where we asked members of different races about their insights as to what can unify Americans. Their answers provide clues as to which values may transcend racial division within our society.

In Search of an American Identity

The notion that we have a unique identity as Americans is not new. In fact, many historians and social theorists (Bercovitch 1981, Fuchs 1995, Gleason 1980, Higham 2001, Lipset 1991, Myrdal 1944, Song 2009, Spiro 2008, R. Williams 1970) have done extensive work on the idea of a unique American identity. These scholars have made the argument that there is an American ideology that binds individuals coming here from other cultures (Gleason 1980, Higham 2001, Lipset 1991, Ravitch 1994). A major proponents of this vision is John Higham (2001), who developed the idea of pluralistic integration as a potential U.S. model. This concept advanced the notion that there is both a common ideology that all groups must subscribe to and also freedom for those groups' own expressions of cultural reality. We accept this concept, but we envision it as a cultural core in which there are common non-material cultural elements that transcend the local concerns of the various racial and ethnic groups in the United States.

While there has been a significant effort toward theorizing what these common cultural elements may be, there has been precious little effort expended to document them. Work has been done to determine how racial or ethnic subcultures have adopted a dominant philosophy (Anagnostou 2009, Connor 1974, Enrile & Agbayani 2007, D. Lewis 2008, Ramos-Sanchez & Atkinson 2009), but this work does not establish what that dominant philosophy is, because of its focus on these subcultures. It is not work that explores the potential cultural agreements across subcultures. Historical work (Bercovitch 1981, Fuchs 1995, Lipset 1991, Ricento 2003) has argued that certain cultural elements (i.e., diversity, individualism, democracy) are part of a greater American ideology, implying that these are values that cross racial and ethnic divides. But such work can only speculate on what that ideology might have been in the past. Our search of academic literature failed to find any work that attempted to empirically answer the question of what constitutes the cultural core in the United States. Robin Williams's famous work (1970) outlining a constellation of American values is based on his observations, not on research occurring where those values are enunciated. Since we do not want anyone to assume that we are attempting to claim that our own particular values are common among Americans, we must find research in which respondents themselves articulate "American" values. Yet, we could not find work that indicated there are common cultural beliefs among Americans across racial and ethnic groups. Without such substantiating research, any contention that a certain value is part of a common cultural core is at best speculation and at worst a projection of one's own cultural values.

A Quick Refresher: Why We Need a Common Core

Getting outside the fishbowl of the United States, present-day Europe shows us what can happen when there is a lack of cultural consensus. Many European countries are struggling to live with Muslim populations that have rejected the secular, humanist tenets of those nations (Nielsen 1999, Rath et al. 2001, Shadid & van Koningsveld 2005, Tibi 2002). Many of the secular, postmodern values of white Europeans clash with the deeply religious beliefs of their immigrant Muslim neighbors. It seems that little effort has gone into discovering what values, if any, these groups share. As a result, the degree of intergroup strife between the Muslim and non-Muslim segments of these countries has recently increased (Fekete 2004, Fetzer & Soper 2005), and may continue to be high for the foreseeable future. We can evade the problem of ethnic, racial, and religious tensions only by discovering the values and concerns that connect distinct racial groups.

Interviews of spouses in interracial marriages[1] indicated that while racial concerns were a legitimate topic of discussion between them, the prerogatives of a given racial group were not allowed to take precedent over the concerns of the family. For example, in remarking about raising their children, this forty-four-year-old black man married to a white woman said:

> You know racial issues are taught to children. All you have to do is watch kids play and you will know they're taught [about racial issues]. They are taught a side—the white side, black side, brown side. We don't teach that here in our family. They must learn all sides.

His concern is that neither majority- nor minority-group members should overly influence his children. He does not feel free to completely emphasize his African American perspective over a majority-group perspective, as he has a multiracial family that must accommodate multiple racial perspectives. The value of a core commitment to one's family can be a powerful incentive influencing people to look at the interests of multiple racial groups.

Likewise, research into multiracial congregations indicates that while culturally based racial differences cannot be ignored, there are mutual obligations that forbid that they be allowed to interfere with pursuing the religious organization's larger goals. For example, DeYmaz (2007) documents the development of the multiracial church he pastors in Little Rock, Arkansas. He also tells the stories of three other multiracial churches. One of those churches is led by Rodney Woo, who discusses confronting majority-group resistance as his church pursued racial diversity:

> An important question to keep in mind, of course, is how the majority group is responding to these changes. . . . This continues to be a primary area of struggle for some of our white members who have been with us throughout the entire transitional process. Sometimes they do not feel appreciated for the amount of sacrifice they have given to the multi-ethnic vision, or they assume they will be in leadership based solely on the longevity of their tenure as a leader. One of the steps we have taken to ensure they remain engaged is to involve them in mentoring emerging nonwhite leaders. In addition, we ask them to share leadership responsibilities, whether in a Sunday School class, as part of a church committee, or in another ministry assignment.

Note that Woo must juggle the needs of his majority-group members with the needs of the minority-group members entering the church. He does this by promoting the minority-group members into leadership while still encouraging members of the majority groups to mentor and co-lead with them. This allows both majority- and minority-group members to have a vested interest in the success of this multiracial endeavor, and to learn to learn to share power. Interestingly, in this case, the majority members learn to share power by feeling incorporated into the process of developing new leaders, even if this means they will eventually have to step down. The overall goal of having a successful church overrides the particular concerns of majority- and minority-group members.

Having a goal that is greater than mere avoidance of conflict forced those in interracial marriages and multiracial congregations to subordinate some of their racial interest for the good of the marriage or congregation. Likewise, this overarching goal helps both majority- and minority-group members to accept their mutual obligations. An exclusive focus on maintaining cultural differences distracts us from understanding the social forces that can work to unite racial groups. While it is important to value racial differences, it is also vital to move toward some degree of cultural and value consensus. Failure to find that consensus eventually leads to intergroup strife.

Research into Finding the Common Core

What values do most people hold in common? We can find these by examining people's definition of "American." Unfortunately, previous researchers have not asked this question. But our study of racially integrated churches does just that.

During our examination of multiracial congregations, we sought to discover the racial and social attitudes of their members by interviewing them. To maintain a useful control group we also interviewed people who attended racially homogeneous congregations. One of the questions we asked was "What do you think unites us as Americans?"[2] This question offers insight into how Americans might be able to create ideological constructs that can be affirmed by members of different races.

Our sample, obviously, was not a random one. Because of the religious bias necessarily present in this sample, we must be mindful of patterns that can be theoretically tied to unique religious expressions. Nevertheless, these interviews offer a rich source of data that we would be foolish to dismiss as we attempt to assess what may create a cultural core that can unite Americans of all races.

What Unites Us

Although about 20 percent of all respondents told us that nothing unified Americans, we did find one concept that was most often discussed by the other 80 percent.[3] That was the concept of freedom. As table 8.1 indicates, freedom was the most popular answer among three of the four racial groups. It was not the most popular answer among African Americans, an issue we will address later in this chapter. But European Americans, Hispanics, and Asian Americans all are highly likely to perceive freedom as an important unifying force.

What did our respondents mean by freedom? Freedom can be broadly defined in two ways. First, it can mean being able to be free

Table 8.1 LSAF participants' primary response to the question "What do you think unites all Americans?" by race (in percent of column total, $N=101$)

Response Category	White ($n=42$)	Black ($n=35$)	Hispanic ($n=8$)	Asian ($n=16$)
Freedom/Liberty	53%	15%	50%	94%
Economic opportunity/Social mobility	5%	3%	–	25%
Nothing	21%	22%	–	6%
Humanitarianism	10%	26%	13%	13%
Social Structure	10%	6%	13%	6%
Crisis	7%	3%	13%	6%
Patriotic Spirit	10%	–	–	–
American Values	5%	3%	–	6%

Note: A total resulting in more/less than 100 is due to rounding error repersents multiple categories in respondents' answers or omission of categories.

from the constraints of one's status, to do as one wants within legal limits, and, through democracy, to decide those legal limits. This is basically a civil liberties mode of freedom. For example, in response to the question of how we might unify Americans, one of the white respondents stated:

> Well, I think everybody in the United States is attached to the notion of freedom. Ah, but I think that, beyond that, I don't think there's much that I would say really would be a unifying thing and certainly it is not Christianity or any one particular religion. But, certainly, I think we're all united around the notion of freedom [and] democracy.

This man emphasizes the idea that our democracy, or the basic freedom to vote and choose our leaders, is a unifying force. It is not religion that is a unifying force, since there are different religions; rather, it is the idea that people of all faiths have access to the same democracy. When individuals simply stated "freedom," as several of them did, we assumed that they were approaching it from this basic idea of democracy, or the freedom to do whatever one desires, within certain legal limitations.

However, we also noticed that some individuals conceptualized freedom as having a certain economic component; that is, more as the opportunity to achieve economic success in our society. An Asian American man notes, "It seems to me like money is something that all Americans gravitate to for success, independence." This answer is a form of the freedom answer, but it focuses on the attainment of material goods.

Thus, while freedom was the common factor that tended to unite the nonblack racial groups, it does come with different conceptual foci. All of the racial groups emphasized the civil liberties notions of freedom more than the economic opportunity so these different definitions are not linked to racially based cultural differences. However, they do remind us that the concept of freedom can have distinct variations in meaning.

Still, we can state with some confidence that one critical concept Americans agree on is the idea of freedom. Desiring freedom is part of what makes one an American in the United States. Those who come here from other countries are likely to either already have a powerful notion of freedom or to develop such a notion from those already living in the United States. Thus, freedom as a core American concept is one that can be accepted easily by multiple racial groups and is not one that has to be imposed upon such groups.

But before we address how this value of freedom can be used to help create a unifying core, we have to address a discrepancy in the data. African Americans were not nearly as likely as members of other groups to claim that freedom is what unites Americans. The importance of the African American community to the eradication of racial alienation in our society is too great for us to ignore. Thus, we must explore more deeply African Americans' ideas about freedom.

African Americans and Ideas about Freedom

The barrier between blacks and whites may be the primary barrier driving racial conflict in our society. While some have argued that focusing on blacks' racial struggles takes attention from the racial issues that other people of color face (Brown & Crompton 1994, T. Cox 2004, Pedraza 2000), much research suggests that the main source of racial alienation in our society is an animus toward African Americans (Gallagher 2004a, Massey & Denton 1996, Mechanic 2005, Yancey 2003b). It would be particularly galling to devise a plan to overcome the racial estrangement in the United States that is implemented at the expense of African Americans.

The unique alienation of African American—from forced immigration to slavery to Jim Crow to segregation and parallel institutions to the taking of black wealth—may help account for why African Americans are less likely than others to see freedom as a unifying force. Given the relative level of ostracism African Americans face, they may be less likely to perceive the United States as a place of freedom.

Within African American thought, the idea of freedom is far from foreign. In fact, much of the trajectory of black thought is how African Americans can gain their freedom from an oppressive society (Andrews 2004, Chafe 1981, M. King 1958, Simms 2001). But while freedom is something to strive for, it is also something often viewed as unattained if not unattainable.

Roberts (2005) explores black theology and, in doing so examines, the notion of liberation. Roberts argues that liberation, rather than freedom, may be a more useful concept since freedom is an idea that has been badly distorted for African Americans. Blacks have experienced the granting of freedom to those of other races while they have repeatedly been denied it themselves, or have had to die to attain a measure of it. Freedom implies that we have arrived; liberation implies the need to revolt against social and institutional constraints to obtain full freedom. The desire for liberation, which can be seen as a type of freedom, may be just as, or even more, powerful among African Americans as it is among those of other races.

Because of the prominence of the black church, it has been the reservoir of African American culture. Advocates of black theology have given the desire for liberation or freedom a central place in the ideology (Cone 1999, Hopkins 2000, Simms 2001). Indeed, the value of freedom or liberation was also a driving force behind the modern civil rights movement, in which African Americans played such a prominent role (Chafe 1981, Lawson 1991). Thus, the desire for freedom is deeply embedded within African American culture.

While the way the ideology of freedom manifests itself within African American culture differs from the way it does so within the cultures of other races, that ideology is clearly evident. Therefore, it is fair to argue that freedom can be a core value that unites people in the United States. Clearly, this is only a start in the effort to discover the unifying values in our society, but we are now confident that the idea of freedom is part of what would comprise a unifying core of U.S. values.

What Does the Core Concept of Freedom Mean?

African Americans' perception of freedom includes the idea of being released from the devastating effects of racial oppression. Majority-group understanding of the idea of freedom is likely connected to the idea of being able to do what one wants.[4] This can be related to the larger differences between whites and blacks in their evaluation of individualism and social structures, those social arrangements within which we live (Blauner 1994, Emerson & Smith 2000, Kluegel 1990). Non-black people of color may have an understanding of freedom that is somewhere in the middle of these two concepts, or they may have a perspective that is distinct from that of blacks and that of whites. Thus, each racial group may conceptualize freedom in distinct ways, but they nevertheless all appeal to the concept of freedom to legitimate their societal desires.

It is fair to argue that a key way to legitimate societal claims in the United States is by claiming the need for freedom. This was seen in the major U.S. civil rights movements, where freedom has consistently been part of the ideology driving them (M. King 2003, R. King 1996, Korstad & Lichtenstein 1988; Lawson 1991). However, we also see an appeal to freedom in the modern claims of social movements overrepresented by white activists, such as the modern feminist (Derrick Bell 1993, Cornell 1998, Fan 1997, Hirschmann 2002) and gun-rights movements (Lio, Melzer, & Reese 2008, Singh 1999, Utter & True 2000) movements.

In this way, freedom is an "American" value that can unite all races, and it is a value that many societies do not value as much. In certain Islamic nations, adherence to the societal religion is more highly valued than is individual freedom or freedom from societal oppression (Afkhami 1995, An-Na'im 1987, Feng & Zak 1999, Karatnycky 2002). In certain Asian nations, the individual is not seen as being as important as the group or as society, and thus freedom is not an overarching value there (Kim 1995, Winfield, Mizuno, & Beaudoin 2000). Our main point is that in the United States freedom is the value that undergirds much of what is seen as desirable and that this valuation of freedom is not a cultural universal.

Since the value of freedom is already powerfully embedded in our society, it can be used to unite. Rather than use it to emphasize only individual rights and freedom from the constraints of others, we can use it to eliminate ideas and cultural concepts that deprive other Americans of freedom. An attack on freedom is an attack on our individual rights, such as freedom of religion or political thought, and an attack that threatens us through structural racism, such as police profiling. Americans of all races have a mutual obligation to discourage anything, no matter what cultural tradition it comes from, that jeopardizes such freedoms. This mutual obligation takes us beyond the trap of multiculturalism, which does not allow us to criticize other cultures. We can, and should, address elements in those cultures that rob others or us of freedoms. One may worry that such criticism may lead to unfair attacks on the traditions of minority cultures. Yet, as we have seen, freedom is so broadly valued as to allow us to find its manifestations in other cultures.

We understand that different individuals and groups may have contrasting ideas about the concept of freedom. Part of developing our societal core will be to address contradictory value claims. For example, some may argue that racial profiling can be an effective way to detect or monitor certain types of crimes. Preventing these crimes allows more freedom for law-abiding citizens. However, many others would point out that profiling by definition robs certain racial groups of the freedom to live without being unnecessarily targeted by law enforcement. People's opposition to profiling is connected to the need to be free from racial oppression, since the profiling is based upon racial differences. We believe that such arguments are necessary so that eventually a global understanding of freedom can develop. As long as the opposing sides of such arguments are encouraged to base their contentions upon the values of freedom, then we will be able to build upon the core values in our society and work toward a society where those core values unify, rather than divide, us.

Of course, we are not proposing the implementation of some formal law or sanction that forces everyone to accept freedom as an important value (such an effort would itself be an affront to freedom). We envision instead a society advocating that to not value freedom is to be somehow "un-American." We see nothing wrong with promoting informal, or social, pressure to encourage people to accept freedom as a value. While such pressure can limit support for certain types of ideologies in our society, it can also help reduce efforts to limit dialog. For example, challenges to patriotism should be based upon the willingness of a person or a group to accept the value of freedom in the United States. Using this criterion lessens the possibility that political and social dissent will be stigmatized with accusations of treason, unless of course if it can be shown that such dissent is connected to an attempt to rob others of their freedom. Furthermore, we believe that Americans of every race can help us develop our notions of freedom by offering their unique interpretations. We should not be limited to merely the interpretations of a single or few racial groups; rather, we envision an ongoing dialogue about what freedom means to various groups and how we can develop this value across the entire spectrum. Such a cognitive project can help unify all groups.

Freedom, of course, is not the only American core value. At this point, we are not able to empirically assess what other values may be core. The research in this chapter is only a beginning to finding new values that can unify the people of the United States. Our concern is that, although much work has been done to document the source of racial divisions, little empirical work has explored the concepts that can unite Americans of different racial groups. We would encourage such work so that a more complete understanding of our cultural core can eventually develop.

Coming Together with Our Cultural Core

While there has been a tremendous amount of historical and theoretical debate about the values embedded in our society, there has been precious little research on this topic. Unfortunately, the lack of research on what composes our cultural core inhibits our current understanding of its composition. We are under no illusion that our work is the final word on what this cultural core may look like. In fact, we hope that by sharing this work we can encourage more research on American cultural unity. With more research, such as that discussed in this chapter, we will gain a deeper understanding of the values that make Americans as a group unique and that can serve to bind us together.

We recognize that work into discovering these core values will not always be straightforward and easy to interpret. It has been suggested that the identity and values in our society are likely to be contrasting and conflicting (Anagnostou 2009, Cerulo 2008, Schildkraut 2002, R. Williams 1970). Indeed, those values may be situational and subject to temporary alterations depending on unique conditions that may arise from time to time (Li & Brewer 2004, Schildkraut 2002). As we have seen with the value freedom, each racial group may have a different interpretation of this value, even though it operates across racial groups. Nevertheless, it is clear that the cultural core remains an overarching ideological framework that produces accountability among racial groups in the United States. Such accountability is necessary if unity is ever going to be possible.

Let us be clear. Emphasizing a common cultural core in the United States can damage the wonderful cultural diversity that characterizes the United States. As we address the construction of the cultural core, we must also find ways to encourage cultural diversity. This is why our last major recommendation for transcending racial alienation is to emphasize the expression of cultural freedom. Diverse expressions that do not violate the agreed-upon core values of our society can allow us to fully experience the best of our shared and separate cultures. They can also help us address resentment from those who may feel trapped by the notion of a cultural core. Thus, in the next chapter, we we focus on the need to encourage unique cultural expression.

NINE

CULTURAL UNIQUENESS

When I (Emerson) was in graduate school, my very first assignment in my first graduate class was this: "Imagine everyone in class had unique bodies but shared the same brain. What would be the outcome? Working alone, tell me in five typed pages." My fellow students and I thought the professor rather odd for giving us such a far-fetched assignment, but being new and dutiful graduate students, we did as we were asked.

We came back to the next class session with our completed assignments and proceeded to discuss them. Interestingly, we all independently came to the same conclusion. If we all had the same brain, social interaction would be impossible. It is only by having at least some difference that we can relate to one other. If we all thought the same thoughts, desired the same things, and had the same values, there would be no purpose in social interaction. We considered whether "the same-brain scenario" ever played out in real life. We decided there were close approximations. In some relationships, one person completely conforms to another's wishes, attitudes, and behaviors. Have you ever observed or experienced this yourself? What happens? People in such situations wither, becoming just shells of human beings. They have to so deny themselves that a self is no longer there. In some sense, they become a clone of the other person.

Clearly, this is not a healthy relationship. In fact, in such a case, it is not a relationship at all. No negotiation remains, no distinct personalities, no unique contributions, no learning from each other, no growth. For a relationship to work, it is clear, people must share things in common—perhaps have similar experiences, agree on the basic meaning and purpose of life, enjoy bowling, or both think the New York Yankees are the devil incarnate. But they cannot share everything in common; they cannot have the same brain. It is this difficult but necessary balance between having commonalities and valuing each other's distinctions that makes a relationship healthy and viable.

It works exactly the same for groups. Groups have their own personalities and ways of doing—what we call culture. For distinct groups to come together, they *must* share a core and they *must* have distinctions. There is no other way. Our students in race and ethnicity classes intuitively recognize this fact. We often take a day or so to discuss the various models describing how racially and ethnically diverse Americans ought to relate to each other. Here are six models:

Table 9.1

Category	Name	Input	Outcome
ASSIMILATION	Anglo Conformity	Group A + Group B	Group A
ASSISIMILATION	The Melting Pot	Group A + Group B	Group C
MUTUALITY	Beef Stew	Group A + Group B	Group C_a + Group C_b
MUTUALITY	Lasagna	Group A + Group B	Group AC + Group BC
MULTICULTURALISM	Tossed Salad	Group A + Group B	Group A_c + Group B_c
MULTICULTURALISM	Mosaic Model	Group A + Group B	Group A + Group B

Note: C = Common Culture

We take the time to explain each model, in context. The official motto of the United States—e pluribus unum (out of many, one)—reveals both an early recognition of diversity, and the hope, vision, and value of unity arising from this diversity. But how this should be worked out in practice has been debated, enforced, and negotiated, and is subject to the vicissitudes of time and circumstance. For most of U.S. history, assimilation dominated, though it varied between strict Anglo conformity—others are welcome, but they must come to be like Anglos in most every way possible—and the melting pot—a new culture shall be created from the many groups, one that is not that of any of the groups (though again, because of white predominance and power, the melting pot looked more white than anything else). As the twentieth century began, multiculturalism gained ground, taking strong hold after the sweeping changes of the 1960s to compete against assimilation, dominating in some institutions such as schools.

There are at least two other possibilities, both of which fall under the rubric of "mutuality." Here, the emphasis is on balancing commonalities and cultural uniqueness. One model might resemble a beef stew, with distinct significant aspects of culture (the beef) surrounded by and seasoned with a greater quantity of vegetables and herbs. In the other mutuality model, both unique cultures and commonalities have equal weight. As in lasagna, then, there are layers of cheese, sauce, and noodles, each independent, each adding and absorbing the flavors of the others, and all contributing, in their uniqueness and their merging, a new dish.

In class, being careful not to bias our explanations of these models, we simply write them up on the board (or these days, present them using PowerPoint), explain them, and then ask which model the students prefer. Almost no one chooses Anglo-conformity or the mosaic model. Occasionally, someone chooses the melting pot or the tossed salad (unique ingredients lightly flavored with a dressing). Most often, the students prefer either the beef stew or the lasagna model. We do not find variation by racial or ethnic group.

These young, bright, diverse students intuitively express that we must have mutuality to have an effective society. They want us to remain diverse, with unique cultures, and to share a common core. Having discussed in the last chapter the common core, what does maintaining cultural uniqueness in such a context actually look like?

Getting Specific

As we noted above, for most of U.S. history, one form or another of assimilation has been the de facto model of "unity in diversity." Most bluntly, achieving unity relied on attempts to squeeze out group distinctiveness. This effort began in the highest office in the land—that of the U.S. president.

"The bosom of America," the first U.S. president, George Washington, said, "is open...to the oppressed and persecuted of all Nations and Religions." But he encouraged immigrants to shed the "language, habits and principles (good or bad) which they bring with them." Let them come not in clannish groups but as individuals, prepared for "intermixture with our people." Then they would be "assimilated to our customs, measures and laws: in a word, soon become one people."[1]

In 1915 President Woodrow Wilson spoke to a group of recently naturalized citizens, saying "You cannot become thorough Americans if you think of yourselves in groups. America does not consist of groups. A man who thinks of himself as belonging to a particular national group in America has not yet become an American."[2] And two years later, President Teddy Roosevelt said in a speech in New York, "We can have no 'fifty-fifty' allegiance in this country. Either a man is an American and nothing else, or he is not an American at all."[3]

Beyond the admonishment of presidents, the United States pushed for assimilation in many other ways. It did so by having one educational system that stressed Western history, Western ideals, Western heroes. It had a political system rooted in Western values and practices, run by whites and those who thought like them. It had an entertainment industry run by whites teaching white values and focusing on white themes (be they conservative or liberal), using whites actors and actresses except when a villain or servant was needed. Even the cartoons featured white heroes and heroines, or were voiced by whites. And certain groups and institutions pushed for assimilation through oppression, ridicule, violence, law, unequal practices, and even on occasion murder. Several of these practices remain, certainly the assumption that U.S. culture is white culture (see chapter 1).

In our contemporary research on interracial families, schools, neighborhoods, houses of worship, and groups, we have found a tendency, when these organizations or groups first form, for the people in charge, whether blatantly or subtly, to encourage and practice some form of assimilation, no matter the rhetoric (see e.g., Christerson, Emerson, & Edwards 2005, Emerson 2006: ch. 6). But we have also found that such groups do not last or work effectively if that tendency continues. So to survive and thrive, at least in the interracial settings we have studied, these groups must implement some model of mutuality.

Yancey, in his book *Interracial Contact and Social Change* (2007b), examines what happens to the racial attitudes of people in intermarriages. He found that while the attitudes of nonwhites do not much change, the attitudes of whites do, becoming more similar to those of their nonwhite spouses. Moreover, in his not-yet-published interviews, he found a pattern of mutuality among interracially married couples on the topic of cultural practices. For example, according to this thirty-five-year-old Hispanic woman married to a white man, when asked whether their marriage had altered their entertainment practices, she responded:

> There's more of a duality we'll go to, I mean, we don't go to too many plays, but when we go to plays we'll go to stuff like the *Lion King*, but then at the same time we'll see, like, theater productions that are with Spanish theater companies in town. So we do a little bit of both. We do a little bit of this and a little bit of that.

A thirty-six-year-old white woman married to a Latino had this to say about cultural practices for holidays:

> What's interesting is that our first Thanksgiving together we had a Mexican Thanksgiving, you know, with the refried bean and the whole works. So, you know, instead of doing things that were more Anglo or typical [for me] we have integrated more types... into what we're doing, so trying to bring more of his background into celebrations.

We find a similar pattern in religious congregations. Whites' attitudes are altered: they become more likely to recognize racial inequality and to be more supportive of racial equality (Emerson & Yancey 2008). In both cases, whites do not stop being culturally white, but they do come to agree with most nonwhites that race is indeed a real issue in the United States and that change is needed.

Embracing one's culture while at the same time being part of an organization with common goals was an issue discussed frequently by those we interviewed in racially mixed congregations. The following discussion with a black woman from an interracial congregation in the Northeast is representative. When asked if she preferred maintaining cultural uniqueness or a common culture or a combination of both, she responded:

> I think there should be something that brings us all together, but I don't think I need to leave something behind in order for me to come together with people. I need to be able to be who I am in all my culturalism and everything, all that I am, I need to continue to be that way, but that doesn't mean I can't hang out with another culture and enjoy the people and have a connection with the people.
>
> *If we should bring the races together, what do you think should bring us together?*

Christ, absolutely. Because he's the only thing that doesn't discriminate. Anything else, there will be some type of bias.

If you have Christ as a common culture, where can you have your distinctiveness?

Our heritage, our traditions. The way we cook, the way we dance. The types of music that we like to listen to.... And just my blackness, no matter how black I want to be and how loud I want to be, I just want to be accepted and be proud and accentuate that.

Reflecting on their involvement in attending interracial congregations, respondents often talked about cultural uniqueness as an advantage for group action and learning. One Hispanic male from Houston reported:

I believe that the races should keep their uniqueness. That's what makes it great. I think that if you have a given racial background and unique-ness and so does your [for example] coworker, you can learn to work together. It makes the overall process a lot richer than if you try to force people into one common race or culture.

And from attempting to worship together, be friends, and get things done together, respondents reiterated a common theme, that there is positive value in all cultures. A Hispanic woman from Houston said:

All cultures are good and every one of them has bad things as well as good things. You need to learn to adapt without losing the culture that you know. I guess what I am trying to say is that it is a matter of respecting the differences between cultures. It is good to maintain the values of every culture because there are very nice things in each culture.

And an Asian American man from an interracial congregation in Los Angeles goes further. Not only is there positive value in other cultures, but there is positive value in learning from other cultures, as he illustrated with a specific example:

One of the things I know when I went to [my interracial congregation], there, the Latins really like to express their love and so there would be a lot of hugs. People would come up to you and give you a hug. At the beginning I was not comfortable with that. I felt like, okay, I was hugging people, but I was hugging only on the exterior not really the whole me. And so I'm comfortable with that now. I think one of the things is that when you have interaction among cultures that you have the ability to be able to take advantage of that.

This man grew up with values and practices common to many Asian cultures. In most Asian cultures, and similar to white American culture, people greet others they do not know well with restraint—a bow, a nod, or a gentle handshake. Embracing another person with a hug is something reserved for those who are well known (at least in white American culture—some Asian cultures do not use hugs), such as close family members and perhaps a few friends. But people of many other cultures find such reserved behavior inappropriate, a sign of dislike or even failing to acknowledge another's humanity. Compared to Asian and white cultures, Latin cultures stress and expect much more personal contact. Whereas the typical white American who does not know a person well will stand three to five feet away from that person during conversation, the typical Latin will stand just six to nine *inches* away. Greetings with hugs are common, as they are signs of acceptance and acknowledgment. This Asian man encountered these two very different cultural expressions of greeting—the one he was raised in and the typical Latin one. His initial reaction to this juxtaposition of cultural norms was surprise and discomfort with the typical Latin's expression. Over time, however, he came to see the value in this type of expression, recognizing it as a way to greet people raised in cultures where hugging acquaintances is appropriate and expected.

So, for most members of interracial congregations, the experience of being with people from a variety of backgrounds leads them to positively value people's distinctiveness, to want to work together to reach a higher goal or to enrich themselves. In this sense, far from leading to assimilation, at least in the overall context of the multiracial congregations we studied, *integration helped people grow more secure in and proud of their cultural identities.*

The work of the sociologist Elaine Howard Ecklund helps us understand these findings.[4] Ecklund argues that Koreans in multiracial congregations have different views of their identities than do Koreans in Korean congregations, that they are able to simultaneously be Korean and American, and that they are able to value others' ethnicities and statuses because their congregations provide a cohesive religious narrative for seeing racial and ethnic diversity as important. As she writes, these mixed congregations provided a "Christian theology or spiritual lens through which to more broadly understand diversity in America society."[5] In these congregations, those in attendance learned that race and ethnicity should be openly discussed and are valuable human characteristics. At the same time, they came to see that race and ethnicity should not form barriers between people. Instead, they should be used to fulfill others, and to see the fullness of God and creation.

This all sounds good. But given our nation's history, and some people's negative experiences in interracial environments, the idea of integration and stressing a common core evokes nausea or, at a minimum, distaste. Integration is often rightly viewed as a cover, as code, for (forced) assimilation. Our past and present have taught us the consequences of such practices. People never have and never will accept being forced to assimilate. It is true that some will choose to assimilate into one culture or another, given the choice, but they must be given the choice.

And so, in a solution of mutual obligation, we need to discuss the necessity of cultural uniqueness specifically. Cultural uniqueness is necessary for group health, for identity, and for the strength of a nation now competing in a world economic climate that includes the increasingly strong European Economic Union, the Chinese move toward capitalism, the growing influence of India and its more than one billion people, and other economic and political conglomerates.

What It Might Look Like

So the question is, what might cultural uniqueness look like? We can think of the distinction between thin ethnicity and thick ethnicity. Many people in the United States who are assimilated practice thin ethnicity. Perhaps they are of German origin, and enjoy eating German food on the holidays, maybe even learning and using some German phrases. Or perhaps they are half white and the other half is fifth-generation Chinese American (on their mother's side), but they have little connection to that culture except when gathering with older relatives. Or perhaps they are of Swedish descent, and enjoy reading the Swedish American newspaper and following the Swedish ski team. In all these instances, ethnicity is thin—these are "Anglicized" Americans recalling at times a bit of their heritage. It costs them nothing but can bring them some pleasure and some connection to others. Mary Waters (1990) wrote that this is the experience for most white Americans.

On the other hand, thick ethnicity entails practicing a culture much more fully and completely. Perhaps the person is an Italian American who speaks Italian fluently, spends lots of time with other Italians, is married to an Italian American, eats mostly Italian food, is a member of several Italian American organizations, travels to Italy periodically, and attends an Italian Catholic parish. Perhaps the person is an African American who lives in a black neighborhood, attends a black church, went to nearly all-black schools, has a distinct dialect, listens mostly to R&B, hip-hop, and gospel, and hangs out almost exclusively with other African Americans. Perhaps the person is a Mexican American who travels back and forth between Mexico and the United States several times a year, has many relatives in both nations, lives a "transnational life," knows only a modicum of English, and finds many American practices of little interest. The ethnicity is thick in these cases not only in the density of its practice, but in the fact that it cannot easily be given up or hidden, so it can, and likely does, have costs. A thick ethnicity also makes it difficult to fully incorporate into a larger, racially and ethnically diverse culture, beyond perhaps the workplace.

As we have already said, we need, in practice, a balance. When we speak of groups being allowed to maintain cultural distinctiveness if they so choose, we do not mean thin ethnicity. We do not fully mean thick ethnicity either, though groups can certainly have a thicker rather than thinner ethnicity if they also share a common core that allows us to work together and construct a web of mutual obligation. Ideally, groups and individuals can remain as distinctive as they desire, as long as they value commitment to the common core and practice working together. Indeed, only a nation with cultural distinctiveness can be fully healthy.

We can think of cultural distinctiveness as cultural checks and balances similar to our political system's checks and balances. Without the checks and balances, we can be led into massive groupthink; make major world political, economic, or cultural gaffs; or simply end up a dull and boring place, which has never been the vision of the United States. What is more, without a system of cultural checks and balances, we end up with the racial problems outlined in this book.

What does it matter how absorbed into a culture a person or group is, if that person or group also agrees with a common core of mutual obligation? It should not matter. Yes, it can make running organizations and institutions more difficult—must public schools educate students in whatever language they or their parents have been speaking? Must they teach them that evolution is essentially true—or essentially false—based on their religious beliefs? This gets messy and complicated fast.

But this points us to an important aspect of our proposed racial solution. We need not, and sometimes should not, maintain the systems we currently have. Let us stay with the educational system as our example. The United States' educational problem is that the public school system was designed to assimilate children and youth, to make them American, when American meant Anglo-conformity or melting pot. We are now trying to retrofit a more multicultural model, which quickly leads us to absurdities, expensive complexities, and compromises. We need not think in such a box.

In a system of mutual obligation that values cultural uniqueness, we could change our educational system to resemble that of England and some other nations. "Public education" would come to mean not one way of educating everyone, but instead could involve publicly funded schools that are taught from a specific worldview. Take religion, for example. As currently structured, "public schools" in the United States do not teach religion. In the new context, as already seen in some nations, a public school can be any kind of school that is publicly funded. It can be a Muslim school, a Jewish school, a school that emphasizes African American history and experiences, a bilingual school, and so on. This model is better suited to supporting cultural uniqueness.

But what then happens to mutuality, to the creation of a core knowledge base? Again, as in other nations, a core curriculum must be taught in all publicly funded schools—say, the English language, a standardized math skill set, and knowledge of at least five other American cultural groups. But each school is free to learn and interpret in the context of its own culture. So, for instance, the federal government may require that evolution be taught as scientific theory, complete with evidence. But in the new, more flexible system designed to value cultural uniqueness in its very structure, if this were a school based on a religious culture, the teacher would be free to also teach the students the implications of the theory for their religious beliefs, and their religious beliefs' implications for understanding the theory.

What is more, such an organization of schools would allow teaching common core values. If these values include "crime is bad," then instead of teaching simply that this is so because it is against the law, or because societies cannot function without the rule of law, as now happens in public schools, schools could actually anchor the core, in this case "crime is bad, law is necessary," to a larger value system—it is against God's will, it upsets the yin/yang system, it makes our group look bad, it brings shame upon our parents and your relatives.

Undoubtedly, our example raises questions. Would we really be American anymore? Do we really want to allow pubic funding for people we may perceive as "religious nuts," or for a school that uses Spanish in its classes much of the time, or for a school that teaches Afrocentric ideas to its students? Yes, we would really want this if (a) we truly value cultural uniqueness and (b) believe at the same time that a core curriculum must be taught. Indeed, in practice, the core curriculum is undoubtedly what would be taught during most of the school day. Even now, private Christian schools, for instance, spend most of their time teaching reading, writing, math, science, geography, and an agreed-upon core curriculum. To that, it adds theology, religious interpretation of ideas, and perhaps chapel attendance.

Across the institutions of society—education, government, economics, and so on—we can have experts think about how to structure these institutions so as to support a common core of mutual obligation and cultural uniqueness. With a framework in place, the particulars can be negotiated and agreed upon through a dynamic process. As people and groups change, so too will the negotiations and systems. It will be messy—for instance, some people might insist that the common core means that only English be spoken in schools, while others will insist that English be just one of three languages that must be taught—but most of public life is messy. Dialogue, debate, negotiation, compromise are the tools of public life. Group interest must be acknowledge, welcomed, and integrated into the process of negotiation. Who has the most power and who has the least must be explicitly acknowledged before discussions begin. And ground rules for neutralizing this power differential will have to be agreed upon, or the discussions cannot begin. Barriers to successful negotiation must be identified—political interests for example—and ways to reduce them must be found. Humans are pretty smart. If they want to, they can find ways to work together for mutual progress.

Conclusion

Our point in this chapter is that we must create a society that has both a common cultural core and acknowledges our mutual obligations, and we must have cultural and individual distinctiveness. That is the model of *e pluribus unum* that we must now strive for. Anything else is something less than the best, as argued in this chapter, which has offered a framework for moving forward. We now turn to the final chapter and provide a fuller discussion of how to move past racial alienation and inequality.

TEN

RACIAL SOLUTIONS FOR A NEW SOCIETY

As we continue to address the aftermath of our racial history and the racialization that has developed from it, we must find solutions that unite rather than divide us. Solutions that appear to benefit one group at the expense of other groups will not produce the consensus needed to address our racial problems. Such solutions may do very good things, temporarily easing racial tensions, revealing racial inequities, promoting opportunities for racial minorities to succeed, and so on. But if these solutions are not widely accepted as legitimate by multiple racial groups, and do not unite us, they will not sustain a racially harmonious society.

We advocate solutions that are not based exclusively on attributing responsibly to either whites or nonwhites. A balanced solution contains within finding common ground between majority and minority groups so that more-practical recommendations can be advanced. These recommendations will thus become part of a self-sustaining approach because they are accepted by majority and minority groups alike.

Our arguments have been mostly theoretical. Now we move beyond the theories to more closely investigate what a mutual-obligations approach might look like in practice. We will give a step-by-step description of a mutual-obligations model. Then we will use affirmative action as an example to illustrate our approach to addressing both white and nonwhite concerns. Finally, we will explore possible public policy suggestions to support this approach toward race relations, paying special attention to the educational and governmental sectors.

Steps in Using a Mutual-Obligations Approach

To address societal problems, we generally want a blueprint for what we are specifically supposed to do. We are both professors who are well read in the field of race and ethnicity. It is tempting for us to create our own blueprint for solutions to racial alienation. But doing so would merely propagate our own biases for potential racial solutions. Those who do not share our biases would reject our blueprint out of hand. And our ideas, like most before them, would lack the support necessary to lessen racial alienation.

Given the arguments we have laid out in the previous chapters, there *is* a possible approach to effectively address racial concerns. It is an approach that will produce widely acceptable answers and a powerful potential for addressing racial alienation. Outlining this approach is more valuable than making arguments about racial issues based on our own racialized understanding.

The first step in addressing any given social problems is to identify the problem. In so doing, we come to understand and accept the fact that we have important issues to address. Often, we attempt to fix social problems without really understanding what the problems are. This is an especially strong tendency when it comes to racial issues, given the powerful motivation for racial groups to represent racial problems in a self-interested way. Thus, we must *first define the racial problem carefully.*

Second, we must *identify the critical core.* Our research to date has indicated that freedom is a critical core value of Americans of all different races. In time, we hope more research will outline other elements of the critical core, but for now we will work with what we have. It becomes important to carefully consider the implications of freedom as we tackle the racial issues before us. To be specific, it is especially vital to understand how the freedoms of whites and non-whites are affected by the decisions surrounding a given racial issue. Since the value of freedom goes to the heart of what makes the United States unique, appeals to this value are vital in the processes of developing solutions.

Third, it is necessary to *recognize the cultural differences at play.* Even a value as highly respected as freedom comes with contrasting interpretations from distinct racial groups. Thus, we should not use our common values to completely smother our cultural distinctions. Rather, there is a need to recognize how our cultural differences influence each racial group's understandings about values within the critical core and the racial problem being addressed. These cultural values may reinforce attitudes that serve the social and economic interests of one or another racial group.[1] But sometimes these values are not directly connected to obtaining some economic or social good from other racial groups, yet still they are vital to the understanding of the social reality of a particular racial group. Many of us do not understand the cultural values of other racial groups as well as we understand our own racial group's cultural values. To this extent, it is vital that whites listen to nonwhites to fully understand why they have certain concerns, and nonwhites must listen to whites to fully comprehend their positions on racial issues. Such listening is essential and has to be done in a manner that is respectful of those in other groups and not merely as a way to further one's own group's arguments.

Next, it is critical that whites and nonwhites *develop ideas and approaches that also address the concerns of other racial groups.* In other words, it is understandable that the bases of the answers whites produce will be rooted in the nonwhite-obligations solutions outlined in chapter 3. However, whites must also understand the perspectives of nonwhites. As they conceptualize solutions to racial problems, they must attempt to address the concerns of nonwhites. Not until whites work to understand the social and economic interests of people of color and their cultural context will they be in a position to postulate a solution that addresses at least some of nonwhites' concerns.

Likewise, we would expect that nonwhites would base their solutions on the principles discussed in chapter 4. However, they must also attempt to take into consideration the interests and cultural concerns of whites. They must advance solutions that address these interests and concerns even if they are formulated by the ideas in white-obligations solutions. Honest attempts by whites and nonwhites to conceptualize solutions that consider the interests and cultural concerns of racial outgroups will lead to each group developing solutions that are more similar than those characterized by a gap between the white-obligations solutions and nonwhite-obligations solutions. Conceptually, they will be solutions much closer to the middle line in graph 3.1 than the current solutions advanced by major racial groups.

Finally, all of those interested in solving the given racial problem should *take these new ideas and work toward a solution that can be accepted by all.* Because these should be solutions more widely accepted than our current solutions, such merging will be easier than if we were to attempt to merge polarizing solutions such as colorblindness and anti-racism. However, there will still be differences between the two groups of solutions that will need to be thought through. With both the groups having to acknowledging up front what is in their group-interest, finding compromises can be done and can produce a stable solution that takes into consideration the interests of both whites and nonwhites.

Enough of Pie in the Sky: An Example of the Affirmative-Action Conflict

It's easy to discuss racial problems abstractly. We must also apply a mutual-obligations approach to real racial problems. Affirmative action is one of the most contentious racial issues of the past half century. In chapter 2 we briefly discussed the conflict that has grown around this issue, and in chapter 3 we saw some of the arguments directed at this program. Those who support nonwhite-obligation solutions perceive it as an unfair program to whites, one that allows nonwhites access to jobs at the expense of whites. Those who support white-obligations solutions favor such programs, given that such programs attempt to overcome racial injustice. How would a mutual-obligations approach address this sticky problem chock full of divided perspectives and intense emotions?

The first step is to more clearly define the problem. So we begin by recognizing that affirmative action is not an easily defined concept. Many Americans conceptualize measures such as set-asides or racial preference for college entry as strictly affirmative-action efforts. While these can be part of an overall program of affirmative action, it is fairer to state that affirmative action represents an approach to help people of color become more fairly represented in occupations and institutions of higher education associated with higher socioeconomic standing. In a very real sense, affirmative action can be seen as an attempted corrective to the historical injustices that have separated whites from nonwhites. How to achieve such a result can greatly vary. Under this definition, advertising programs that include efforts to reach nonwhite ethnic communities can be considered affirmative action, as can programs such as the more intrusive set-asides. Once we understand that affirmative action is, at its root, an attempt to neutralize the societal disadvantages of people of color, we can see that it is generally in the interest of whites to downplay the vitality of this program. This is so because such programs limit some of their racial advantages, shifting those advantages to people of color. Thus, it is also advantageous for nonwhites to use this program to gain as many advantages as they can, even at the expense of whites.

The next step in a mutual-obligations approach is to recognize that there is an overarching goal to address. If we accept the idea of freedom, in all of its various forms, as a key overarching goal in the United States, then we have to ask whether affirmative action interferes or supports that goal. Advocates supporting white-obligation solutions can argue that affirmative action may help produce more freedom for people of color because such programs help minorities overcome economic and educational barriers. Advocates of nonwhite-group obligations may argue that affirmative action inhibits the freedom of whites to achieve, and their right to hire whomever they see best fit for a position. Both are valid arguments that must be respected, because they represent the very real interests of whites or nonwhites. It is too tempting to dismiss one argument or the other in support of our own group's interest (rather than consider the interest of the community or nation as a whole). But in adopting a mutual-obligations approach, we must always guard against ignoring the interests of those in racial out-groups.

After both arguments are laid out, then we can ask whether the overall effect of affirmative action enhances or detracts from freedom in the United States. For the sake of argument, let us suppose that, generally, affirmative action benefits nonwhites at the expense of whites. If it is the case that affirmative action takes away more freedom from whites than it provides freedom to people of color, we should avoid it.

But if it provides more freedom to nonwhites than the amount of freedom it takes from whites, then it is a net benefit and should be maintained. Of course, this simple assertion does not end the problem. Different groups will come up with different arguments as to what affirmative action does and how to measure how much freedom is gained or taken away. How do we move forward as we argue over this controversial program?

At this point, we must remember that affirmative action does not consist of any single program. There is a variety of ways in which the goals of affirmative action are achieved. We have already commented that advertising in nonwhite ethnic communities is a type of affirmative action. This action may take opportunity from whites, as they have to compete with nonwhites who did not before know about a job or a place at a university. However, most individuals would not consider such a loss of freedom to amount to anything near the freedom gained by people of color's becoming aware of such new opportunities. At the other extreme is a growing consensus that strict quotas should not be part of an affirmative-action program. Finding individuals of a certain racial group to fit some pre-set quota implies a strict loss of whites' freedom that is not offset by the freedom gained by nonwhites. This reality is particularly apparent if the person hired is clearly incompetent. At that point, that person of color is not gaining more freedom, as he or she is unable to fully take advantage of the opportunity provided.

At the extreme margins of affirmative action it becomes relatively easy to see how an overarching standard enables us to develop a program best suited for addressing racial animosity. Including affirmative-action techniques such as advertising to nonwhite ethnic communities and excluding those such as strict quotas leads to a program more acceptable to a large number of Americans. But it is in the disputed aspects of the program, such as timetables and set-asides, that it becomes difficult to find common ground. It is here that we must take into account the third step: compensating for the different cultural values that racial groups bring into the common core. Understanding how whites and nonwhites have contrasting ways of perceiving different mechanisms within affirmative action is needed if we are to find ways to agree on what affirmative-action programs should look like.

Let's consider set-asides, the practice of designating a portion of a government contract for minority-owned businesses. For example, if the government decides to build a bridge, it might stipulate that at least 20 percent of money must go to construction contracts with minority-owned firms. Whites may look at such a practice as being unfair and infringing on their freedom to compete for the full bridge contract. People of color may see set-asides as a way to compensate for their historically being denied the opportunity to obtain such work and for their having been excluded from the social networks and knowledge bases needed to successfully bid on contracts.

To move forward, we have to appreciate that whites tend to a have cultural value called "individualism," which problematizes the notion that anyone be given an advantage because of what has happened to them historically. This value informs whites that only what a business currently bids should matter, not whether there are historical inequities that have created our contemporary situation. However, many groups of color are from high-context cultures (Hall & Hall 1990, Hofstede

1980, Ibarra 1999), meaning that they view social and historical structures as interconnected. Thus, we cannot understand contemporary
racial situations without taking into account the historical context that
has helped produce them. People of color have cultural, and economic, reasons for advocating set-asides as a solution to historical
racism.

So, how do we address the controversial topic of set-asides? What
we do *not* do is what has so often been done before—attempt to push a
solution that exclusively benefits whites or nonwhites. We must stop
seeing this as a competition in which one side wins and the other side
loses. Rather, we must move to facilitating serious discussions among
the affected actors. Both whites and nonwhites should advance their
solutions. However, whites must discuss how their solution addresses
the concerns of nonwhites, and nonwhites must discuss how their
solution addresses the concerns of whites. This means that both whites
and nonwhites must listen to the concerns of those not in their group
and take those concerns seriously. They must both attempt to comprehend the cultural forces that help shape the responses of other racial
groups. In this way, neither group can advocate a solution that meets
only their own social and economic interests. This helps us see the
fourth step in action—whites and nonwhites working on solutions that
address the concerns of other racial groups.

For instance, if whites wish to push for an end to set-asides, then
they must address how they are going to help people of color overcome the historical effects of the racialized society that has robbed
many of them of the ability to compete on a level playing field. If they
have listened, and appreciated the importance of historical context
within cultures of color, then they will not be so quick to dismiss the
concerns of the historical effect of racism. On the other hand, people of
color who want to maintain the current system of set-asides also have
to address the concern whites have about individual merit. They may
have to build within their solutions ways in which set-asides do not
lead to contracts with inferior businesses. If people of color listen
carefully to whites' concerns, then they will take seriously the values
of ahistorical meritocracy embedded in white culture.

Finally, we must take a final step, struggling to merge these solutions
to find widely accepted answers. Solutions developed by whites and
nonwhites under such conditions will not be identical but will be
much more similar than the stark take-it-or-leave-it choice today
offered for set-asides. This struggle will eventually lead to a solution
more easily accepted by individuals of all racial groups. That is the sort

of legitimacy necessary to discover mutual solutions that ameliorate, rather than deepen, racial animosity.

One may ask who will be involved in this conversation. A mutual-obligations approach is about a philosophy that takes into consideration the social and economic interests and cultural differences of those in other racial groups. Ideally, whenever there is discussion among policymakers and influential leaders on how to address racial problems, individuals will feel social pressure to take a mutual-obligations approach. Of course, this is a free country and people can use any approach that they want to when addressing social problems. In no way do we expect legislation or formal rules to govern how people discuss racial issues. However, widespread adoption of a mutual-obligations approach can exert social pressure to devise better solutions. We will discuss possible ways of practically applying this approach later in this chapter. But before we can find ways of using this approach in real life, we have to convince a large segment of society of its value. It is our hope that just as people feel social pressure today to not factor racial superiority into their discussions of racial issues, they will eventually come to feel social pressure to consider the interests of those of other races as they address racial issues.

The potential of a mutual-obligations approach is not limited to addressing affirmative action. Allow us to imagine the result of this approach on other important racial issues. As we consider immigration, it will become important to weigh the very real but unique interests of of various racial and ethnic groups. In hate-crimes legislation, it will be important to balance the interests of multiple groups. With educational reforms, we have to take into consideration both the historical context and the present-day needs of people in different groups. The list can go on. We do not offer specific solutions to any of these dilemmas, but we argue that the approach we have laid out is an important way in which to develop solutions and lessen racial division and inequality as we move toward a truly racially just society.

Public Policy Suggestions

Attempting to work through a cultural core and taking into consideration the perspectives of those of other races can occur regardless of public policy. However, public policy can be altered in a few ways to help bring the mutual-obligations approach into the mainstream. In the rest of this section, we address the possibilities of developing the mutual-obligations approach in educational and governmental sectors, although future work should also consider other societal institutions (economic, religious, etc.).

In our educational system, curriculum development can be used to buttress a mutual-obligations approach. We need curricular material and courses that focus on conflict-resolutions skills and racial attitudes. The materials should come in the form of textbooks written from a solutions-oriented perspective and from the development of educational exercises that help students think about mutual-obligations approaches.

Ideally, instructors will guide students though racial problems and help them see how they can find solutions addressing the concerns of majority and minority groups. Such instructors should consider developing courses in race and ethnicity that incorporate the elements of this approach in their work. For example, such courses could lay out the racial problems by exploring the historical and contemporary context of our racial struggles. They can honestly assess the perspectives and cultures of different racial groups as they pertain to racial issues. They can then help students consider what is unifying among all racial groups and how these values shape our racial debates. Finally, the instructors can help students think about solutions that take into consideration the contrasting social and cultural interests of different racial groups.

It will take time to fully implement an educational mutual-obligations approach. But once implemented, this educational approach will allow us to create an emerging cohort of individuals oriented toward using this approach. These individuals will be the leaders who enable us to address racial problems in a way that reinforces our commonalities even as it recognizes the real differences between groups.

Beyond educational alterations, it is also possible to postulate about a mutual-obligations approach within the framework of our government. For example, as issues of race and ethnicity arise in governmental dealings, there should be interracial committees to develop solutions to those issues. Since we can find people of all different races to support either white-obligation or nonwhite-obligation solutions, these committees must contain ideological and racial diversity. But such committees must not merely devise a single solution. Such a mandate would encourage one group to impose its desires on other groups. Rather, the charge of the committees should be to develop a range of solutions. Connected to each solution should be an assessment of how these solutions will affect both whites and nonwhites.

This may be more clearly seen by looking at a very real problem. The issue of immigration has captured the attention of our society. Perhaps a congressional or presidential committee can be established to investigate which types of reforms are most likely to produce a desired outcome with a minimum of intergroup animosity. This committee would have to be racially and ideologically diverse, which would likely result in its rejecting extreme solutions (e.g., remove all undocumented workers, or open our borders to whoever can cross it). Between those extremes, the committee would develop a variety of potential programs for handling immigration issues. With each solution, the committee would have to outline the effect on immigrants (and their families), as they are the groups most arguably invested in this issue, and on the U.S. born of each of the racial groups. Every program would produce a mix of benefits and costs for each group. The presentation of these options would allow people to debate whether the costs to immigrants and their families were greater than the benefits to U.S. born and vice versa. Such an approach allows policymakers to make a more-informed decision about how to revise our current immigration policy so that it's acceptable to all.

The use of these committees will help blunt the attacks of extremists on all sides of the obligations divide, because the mutual obligations approach the committees use is designed to eliminate solutions which are most biased toward one group or another. The committees and the approach will not eliminate extremist attacks, but they will expose them as untenable. As more Americans begin to appreciate the value of finding solutions respected across racial lines, it will become clearer that advocates of the most viral forms of white-obligation and non-white-obligation solutions will not best serve our nation. The government thus must model a mutual-obligations approach and encourage the rest of us to live up to the best, instead of the worst, in our nature.

Possible Empirical Extensions

If we are serious about using the mutual obligations approach, we must have better understanding of the critical core in the United States. We need to know if freedom is truly part of that core and how it may manifest itself in distinct cultural ways. We must also investigate other possible cultural values that may be part of this critical core. To get at this we can envision a research project that interviews people of different races about their "American" values. Such a project would go much deeper than the single question we used in our previous research and would more fully map the cultural differences, or lack thereof, between racial groups. Once we have a firmer grasp on important cultural core values it will be easier to envision how these values influence racial issues.

Much research already documents how whites and nonwhites interpret racial issues (Blauner 1994, Emerson & Smith 2000, Kinder & Sanders 1981, Kluegel 1990, Schuman et al. 1997). However, we lack work documenting how well members of certain racial groups understand the ideas of other racial groups. The dearth of such work makes it nearly impossible to determine the type of conditions under which people from each racial group are more likely to consider the values and concerns of those of another group. A mutual-obligations approach mandates that people learn to respect and appreciate the views of racial out-groups. We need research illustrating the conditions under which people are more able to respect others' racial views. Once we understand those conditions, we will be in a position to aid those who wish to understand the racial out-groups' perspectives.

Finally, it would be useful to study how both group-interest is exercised and how consensus develops in interracial groups. For example, do whites dominate the group, or do they defer to nonwhites on racial issues and thus shut themselves out of the process? Studying several sets of interracial groups who confront racial problems can provide insight into the patterns emerging from such interactions. This work can make it easier to train people who join interracial groups or committees set up to address racial issues. Researchers conducting such work will be in a position to inform us about whether, and how, interracial groups reach compromises that help both whites and nonwhites and under what conditions such groups are most likely to succeed.

Conclusion

The steps we advocate will come at a cost to both whites and nonwhites. Whites will lose their ability to ignore the fundamental social structures that perpetuate racial inequality. Nonwhites will lose their ability to fix all of the blame for their problems on majority-group members. When the groups come together to resolve their differences, finding compromises often involves a cost. If we focus on the costs of developing mutually acceptable solutions to racial alienation, then we are unlikely to make the effort necessary to live out those solutions. This hesitation to pay the costs is an important barrier that Americans of all racial groups have to overcome.

But there are massive benefits to be gained when there is a real connection between majority and minority groups. For example, whites will be able to express their own racial frustrations without being accused of being racist. With a core that binds all of us, regardless of race, whites will have just as much a right to demand that nonwhites abide by that core as nonwhites will have to demand that whites abide by it. The dreaded "playing of the race card" will be discarded as whites and nonwhites work together, rather than at cross-purposes. On the other hand, nonwhites will be able to communicate their racial frustration to whites and to gain traction in overcoming the historical effects of racism. The burden of generating racial equality will be greatly lessened when whites offer support, instead of resistance, to reach that goal.

It is tempting to argue that addressing alterations to social relationships and attitudes neglects addressing the institutional forces that support racial inequality. But these steps to reduce racial alienation are not a replacement for efforts to address economic and social inequality. Rather, they complement such efforts. Without readjusting by taking steps to reach a balanced solution, it is unlikely that our society will find the willpower to challenge the social structures that buttress racialization in the United States. We offer a mutual-obligations model that supplies us with the rationale needed to motivate whites to address institutional racism but also requires people of color to consider the concerns of whites. If critics of the mutual-obligations model truly fear that its implementation will interfere with attempts to address institutional racism, then we ask that they give the model a chance before succumbing to such fears. Previous efforts have clearly failed to gain the needed consensus to overcome institutional racism; perhaps consensus-building can succeed where raw activism has failed.

Race relations have been dominated by competing self-interest groups. The actual issues have changed, but the pattern of whites and nonwhites fighting each other remains the same. What is more, the general racial order—whites at the top, blacks and Native Americans at the bottom, and other groups located somewhere in the uncertain middle, has been identical since 1776. People of color must use their voice to make sure that their interests are addressed. But their voice is not, nor will it ever be, the only one to be heard. Both whites and nonwhites need a degree of comfort in whatever strategy to dismantle our racialized society we undertake. It is a mutual-obligations approach that will reduce racial alienation and work to undue the racialized society. Our task now is to get to work, so that the next generation might only turn to their history books to learn of racialization and racism, those sad concepts that once were used to carry out injustices.

NOTES

Introduction

1. We had students in a race and ethnicity class read a draft of this book and write a reaction to it. Several white students, but no students of color, mentioned how much they agreed that it is hard to be white these days, that whites are always blamed for problems, and that they often feel like they have to walk on eggshells so as to not offend any people of color. Several white students noted that while racism existed in the past against groups such as Hispanics and African Americans, today, reverse racism seems much more common.

2. Along these lines, see, for example, the work of Tyrone Forman and his colleagues (2004, 2006).

3. For an excellent review of whiteness studies and sources, see Korie L. Edwards (2008).

4. The list of sources is far too extensive to give here, and if we tried, we would most certainly miss many. As a few examples, see Bonilla-Silva 2003; Emerson & Smith 2000; Feagin 2005; and Yancey 2003b.

Chapter 2

1. The Indian Removal Act was intended to force all Native Americans to move west of the Mississippi River. While many Indians tribes agreed to go in order to avoid conflict, the Cherokee resisted, using the American court system to protest the act. Even though they won the case, President Jackson ignored the orders of the Supreme Court and used troops to conduct a forced march of the Cherokee from the Deep South states to Oklahoma. This forced march has commonly been called the "Trail of Tears."

2. The Dawes Act removed the Indian reservations from the control of Native American tribes, who had used the land for the community as a whole, and parceled the land out to individual tribe members because the federal government thought that the tribes were enforcing a communal type of living that inhibited the efforts of Native Americans to develop a "rugged individualism" compatible with European American society. It was also hoped that these individuals would use their land to become farmers. This effort was clearly seen as a way to negate important elements of Native American culture.

3. Richard Pratt infamously described such efforts as attempts to "kill the Indian, and save the man."

4. This tendency to label Hispanics ignores the fact that most of them were at least partially European. Evidently, having some European heritage was not enough to offset the possible Indian and black ancestry of many Hispanics. Thus, the power of white supremacy to oppress nonwhites is more powerful than any particular sympathy that majority-group members might have had toward partially European individuals.

5. This act, passed in 1882, forbids the importation of Chinese into the United States. It marks the first time that a ban on human importation was enacted against a specific race of people.

6. This act forbid Japanese from holding for more than three years any land that they had purchased. Although this was only a state act, it was a state act in California, where perhaps the highest number of Japanese American farmers lived at the time. Thus, this act affected Japanese Americans much more powerfully than it would have in another state.

7. Although there was no evidence of Japanese American sabotage at that time, this lack of evidence, ironically, was used to justify the creation of these internment centers. It was argued that the lack of evidence of sabotage was proof that there was a secret Japanese plot to cripple the United States (DeWitt 1942, Warren 1942).

8. For an even better understanding about this sort of intergenerational transfer see Oliver and Shapiro (1995) treatment of wealth. They clearly show that African Americans are in a more vulnerable position that whites in a similar income level because they have not received wealth from their parents to the same extent as whites. This work demonstrates that even people of color who have a similar level of income to whites are still less likely to possess financial stability. We contend that it may also be true that people of color are also less likely to have inherited positions of authority from their parents than whites.

Chapter 3

1. We do not have to go any further than to remember Martin Luther King's famous line "I have a dream that my four little children will one day live in a nation where they will not be judged by the color of their skin but by the content of their character." While some, such as Dyson (2000), argue that it is inaccurate to argue that King was advocating a colorblind solution, it is still

accurate to state that most individuals interpreted such statements, and the civil rights movement in general, as a call for eliminating racial designations as a factor in how we treat one another. Regardless of what King meant when he made the statement, certain people have interpreted it to support the idea that the best way to address racism is to ignore race.

2. This perspective had been termed "modern racism" (McConahay 1986). However, at this point we do not want to pass judgment on this perspective and will refrain from using this term.

3. In truth, affirmative action is a program used to compensate for both sexism and racism. For the sake of our argument, we will look at it only as it applies to people of color. However, it should be noted that some researchers have observed that the application of affirmative action to racial minorities receives less support than its application to women (Pincus 1996, Sidanius et al. 2000). Thus, our attempt to examine the effects of affirmative action as it applies to people of color allows us to look at the most controversial application of the program.

4. The 2009 Supreme Court ruling supporting the white New Haven firefighters can be used to support this assertion. In that case, the white firefighters sued the city for throwing out a promotion test whereby seventeen whites and two Hispanics, but no blacks, would be promoted. The majority opinion of the court was that this action, which was taken to avoid an disparately adverse effect upon black firefighters, ended up discriminating against white firefighters. Advocates of colorblindness use the case to show how efforts to reverse historical racism can unfairly discriminate against majority-group members.

5. This attempt was a proposition entitled the "Racial Privacy Initiative" and it was soundly defeated in 2003 by a 64 percent to 36 percent margin.

Chapter 4

1. To illustrate the degree of criticism Ignatiev has toward members of the majority group, it is worth noting that he discusses the concept of abolishing the white race from within. Of course, this is not a reference to suicide but rather to the idea that dominant-group members must surrender their previous advantages in the pursuit of racial justice. Ignatiev and Garvey (1996) use the example of John Brown, who was a man of great wealth and prestige but gave it, and his life, up to fight against slavery and for racial justice.

2. There are some advocates of CRT who argue that even this integration is an illusion because the United States is on a path toward resegregation (Orfield & Eaton 1996), even as we pat ourselves on the back for our efforts to promote racial diversity.

3. One way to distinguish between multiculturalism and cultural pluralism is to note that multiculturalism represents the practical application of the philosophy of cultural pluralism.

4. Nihilism is a philosophical concept with complex and varied implications. For our purposes, we will envision nihilism as the loss of the previously

held values and meaning that the African American culture once had. Thus, West is arguing that interaction with the dominant society is corrupting the African American community by stripping it of its cultural foundations, leaving a sense of hopelessness and meaninglessness.

Chapter 5

1. Many millions of Americans find the concept "equality of outcome" a bankrupt concept and an invalid goal. The United States is a meritocracy of individuals. If we had equality of group outcome, or equality of individual outcome, we would not have a meritocracy. That would be un-American.

2. Many readers at this point are crying out, "But it's not that simple—there are not just two perspectives. Lots of people are in the middle somewhere, or don't give it any thought, or . . . " Such readers are correct. The world is more complicated and nuanced than we describe it here. But that doesn't matter. The people in the middle, those who don't care, and the many other less-subscribed-to views are noise in a clear, loud, persistent argument between two giant sides. It is the two perspectives we discuss that make the news, that drive policy perspective and public opinion. Think Democrat, Republican, and the many other political parties in the United States. It is true that there are many political parties—the Green Party, the Socialist Party, the Libertarians, and so on—but 99 percent of the time it is the Democrat or the Republican who wins the election. In the name of clarity and appropriate focus, we chose to ignore the vast but minimal role of the diversity of other perspectives, at least for now.

3. Niebuhr 1932.

4. Niebuhr 1932:xxii–xxiii.

5. Hechter 1987:41.

Chapter 6

1. It is tempting to write off this research with an argument of self-selec-tion—which is that individuals who are more racially tolerant are more likely to engage in interracial contact. Therefore, it is unclear whether interracial contact has created positive racial attitudes or the positive racial attitudes preceded the interracial contact. While this remains a possibility, there have been a sufficient number of studies that have taken self-selection into account and still document contact effects (Dixon & Rosenbaum 2004, Ellison & Powers 1994, T. F. Pettigrew & Tropp 2000) for us to have confidence that self-selection cannot be the only cause of the interracial-contact effect.

2. As noted earlier, there are quantitative studies that indicate that contact effects are not driven merely by self-selection. Yancey's observation merely reinforces these previous assertions.

3. However, even those in such areas still have access to people of other races through online social networks and Web sites such as MySpace and Facebook.

4. Yancey (2003a) has found that, ironically, multiracial churches are more likely to grow than are single-race churches. Thus, the homogeneous-church ideal makes sense theoretically, but it does not hold up empirically.

5. This may also be a reason that, according to research, multiracial marriages have more potential for altering racial attitudes than do interracial intimate friendships (Yancey 2007b). In marriage, the spouses likely share the goal of creating a successful family, whereas such a powerful core commitment is probably lacking in many close friendships. Without this commitment, individuals who are merely friends are free to joke about or ignore race, as noted by Korgen (2002). Although we have no empirical evidence to support such an assertion, future research may be used to evaluate the accuracy of it.

6. Of course, there is also a certain degree of cultural agreement reflected in a society's laws.

Chapter 7

1. Earlier in the interview the pastor had established that the leadership structure of the church was one in which, technically, the elder board possesses the same degree of decision-making ability as the pastor. While this is unlikely the case in the decisions that are actually made, it is worth noting that diversifying the elder board of the congregation put people of different races into key decision-making positions.

2. There is a school of thought stating that religious organizations that concentrate on only one or a few racial subcultures are more likely to grow than are those that spread themselves too thin (McGavran 1990, Wagner 1979, 1996). The work supporting this idea has been disputed (Emerson 2006, Pocock & Henriques 2002, Yancey 2003a), but even if it were true it would not be applicable to multiracial congregations. These congregations have already been able to grow with a racially diverse laity; thus, concentration upon a single racial group is much more likely to depress the number of congregants than it is to increase them.

3. Obviously, this should not be taken to mean that racial groups are unable to ever consider their own group interest. Because of ethnocentrism, it is likely that most people will always value their own group interest over that of other racial groups. However, we do contend that it is important that people are taught to at least add the consideration of others' social interests into their decisions, so that solutions to racial problems that do develop reflect the concerns and interests of several racial groups.

Chapter 8

1. To see the methodology of this research, see Yancey (2007a).

2. We also asked the respondents "What do you think divides us as Americans?" It is possible that the answers to this question may indicate sources of social agreement between members of different races; however, we were

more interested in documenting what unites races than discovering what they all tend to find troubling.

3. We are indebted to Douglas George (and Yancey, 2009) for his preliminary analysis of this data. He is the lead author of a more complete assessment of this question.

4. Indeed, there is research indicating that we have developed a postmodern society that highly emphasizes removing the traditional societal constraints on people's actions (Daniel Bell 1992, Harris 2003a, Thomson 1989). While we could not find any research examining whether some races are more inclined than others to accept a postmodern ideology, there is work that suggests that there are powerful age effects, with younger people being more likely than older individuals to accept this ideology (A. Harris 2003, Ortner 1998, Sacks 1996). It is quite plausible that this age effect will, in time, overpower any potential racial difference, in that younger people, regardless of their race, will tend to have a high degree of postmodern ideology.

Chapter 9

1. Quoted in Schlesinger Jr. (1992: 30).

2. From a speech by Woodrow Wilson delivered May 10, 1915, in Philadelphia (Wilson 1924: 115–116).

3. From a speech delivered September 10, 1917 (Woodrow Wilson 1931: ch. 21, p. 38).

4. See Ecklund's work *Korean American Evangelicals: New Models for Civic Life* (2006). We draw particularly but not exclusively from chapter 4 of this work. See also Ecklund (2005).

5. Ecklund (2006: 81).

Chapter 10

1. A clear example of this can be seen in the research on white racial identity (Dyer 1997, Hartigan Jr. 1999, Twine 1997). This research documents how such a racial identity has developed to support the interests of whites even though they propagate values that seem to be racially neutral.

REFERENCES

Afkhami, Mahnaz, ed. 1995. *Faith and freedom: Women's human rights in the Muslim world.* I. B. Tauris.

Allport, Gordon. 1958. *The nature of prejudice.* Anchor.

Amir, Yehuda. 1976. The role of intergroup contact in change of prejudice and ethnic relations. In *Towards the elimination of racism,* ed. Phyllis Katz, 245–308. Pergamon.

An-Na'im, Abdullahi A. 1987. Religious minorities under Islamic law and the limits of cultural relativism. *Human Rights Quarterly* 9:1–18.

Anagnostou, Yiorgos. 2009. A critique of symbolic ethnicity: The ideology of choice? *Ethnicities* 9(1):94–122.

Andrews, Kenneth T. 2004. *Freedom is a constant struggle: The Mississippi civil rights movement and its legacy.* University of Chicago Press.

Anner, John. 2004. Have the tools at hand: Building successful multicultural social justice organizations. In *Race, class and gender: An anthology,* ed. Margaret L. Andersen and Patricia H. Collins, 542–52. Wadsworth.

Ansell, Amy E. 2008. Paying for the past: Prospects and obstacles facing reparations politics in the U.S. and South Africa. In *Globalization and America: Race, human rights, and inequality,* ed. Angela J. Hattery, David G. Embrick, and Earl Smith, 83–101. Rowman & Littlefield.

Arab American Anti-Discrimination Committee. 2003. *Report on hate crimes and discrimination against Arab Americans.* ADC.

Aronson, Elliot. 1992. *The social animal.* W. H. Freeman.

Aveling, Nado. 2002. Student teachers' resistance to exploring racism: Reflections on 'doing' border pedagogy. *Asia-Pacific Journal of Higher Education* 30:119–30.

Awan, Mazhar A. 1997. Educational development in the black community. In *Black and right: The bold new voice of black conservatives in America*, ed. Stan Faryna, Brad Stetson, and Joseph G. Conti, 51–57. Praeger.

Barak, Gregg. 1991. Cultural literacy and a multicultural inquiry into the study of crime and justice. *Journal of Criminal Justice Education* 2:173–92.

Barnard, William A., and Mark S. Benn. 1988. Belief congruence and prejudice and ethnic relations. *Journal of Social Psychology* 128 (February): 125–34.

Baron, Dennis. 1990. *The English-only question: An official language for Americans?* Yale University Press.

Bash, H. M. 1979. *Sociology, Race and Ethnicity*. Gordon & Brench.

Bell, Daniel. 1992. The coming of the post-industrial society. In *The postmodern reader*, ed. Charles Jencks, 250–66. St. Martin's Press.

Bell, Derrick. 1993. *Faces at the bottom of the well: The permanence of racism*. Basic Books.

Bell, Linda A. 1993. *Rethinking ethics in the midst of violence: A feminist approach to freedom*. Rowman & Littlefield.

Bennett, William J. 1994. *The devaluing of America*. Thomas Nelson.

Bercovitch, Sacvan. 1981. The rites of assent: Rhetoric, ritual, and the ideology of American consensus. In *The American self: Myth, ideology and popular culture*, ed. Sam B. Girgus, 5–45. University of New Mexico Press.

Berkhofer, Robert F. 1979. *The white man's Indian*. Vintage.

Blauner, Bob. 1994. Talking past each other: Black and white languages of race. In *Race and ethnic conflict: Contending views on prejudice, discrimination and ethnoviolence*, ed. Fred L. Pincus and Howard Ehrlich, 18–28. Westview.

Bobo, Lawrence. 1983. White opposition to busing: Symbolic racism or realistic group conflict? *Journal of Personality and Social Psychology* 45:1196–1210.

————. 2000. Race and beliefs about affirmative action: Assessing the effects of interests, group threat, ideology, and racism. In *Racialized politics: The debate about racism in America*, ed. David O. Sears, Jim Sidanius, and Lawrence Bobo, 137–64. University of Chicago Press.

Bobo, Lawrence, James R. Kluegel, and Ryan A. Smith. 1997. Laissez-faire racism: The crystallization of a kinder, gentler, antiblack ideology. In *Racial attitudes in the 1990s: Continuity and change*, ed. Steven A. Tuch and Jack K. Martin, 15–42. Praeger.

Bonilla-Silva, Eduardo. 1997. Rethinking racism: Toward a structural interpretation. *American Sociological Review* 62:465–80.

————. 2001. *White supremacy and racism in the post–civil rights era*. Lynne Rienner.

————. 2003. *Racism without racists: Color-blind racism and the persistence of racial inequality in the United States*. Rowman & Littlefield.

————, and Amanda Lewis. 1999. The new racism: Toward an analysis of the U.S. racial structure, 1960s–1990s. In *Race, ethnicity and nationality in the United States: Towards the Twenty-first century*, ed Paul Wong, 55-101. Westview.

Briggs, Xavier de Souza. 2003. Bridging networks, social capital, and racial segregation in America. Working Paper Series 38, Harvard University Faculty, John F. Kennedy School of Government.

Brooks, Roy L. 2004. *Atonement and forgiveness: A new model for black reparations.* University of California Press.

Brown, Kendrick T., Tony N. Brown, James S. Jackson, Robert M. Sellers, and Warde J. Manuel. 2003. Teammates on and off the field? Contact with black teammates and the racial attitudes of white student athletes. *Journal of Applied Social Psychology* 33(7).

Brown, Phillip, and Rosemary Crompton. 1994. *Economic restructuring and social exclusion.* Routledge.

Brown, Tony N., James S. Jackson, Kendrick T. Brown, Robert M. Sellers, Shelley Keiper, and Warde J. Manuel. 2003. There's no race on the playing field: Perceptions of racial discrimination among white and black athletes. *Journal of Sports and Social Issues* 27(2):162–83.

Butler, John Sibley. 2005. *Entrepreneurship and self-help among black Americans: A reconsideration of race and economics.* State University of New York Press.

Carr, Leslie G. 1997. *Color-blind racism.* Sage.

Cerulo, Karen A. 2008. Social relations, core values, and the polyphony of the American experience. *Sociological Forum* 23(2):351–62.

Chafe, William Henry. 1981. *Civilities and civil rights: Greensboro, North Carolina, and the black struggle for freedom.* Oxford University Press.

Chavez, Linda. 1991. *Out of the barrio: Toward a new politics of Hispanic assimilation.* Basic Books.

Childs, Erica C. 2005. *Navigating interracial borders: Black–white couples and their social worlds.* Rutgers University Press.

Christerson, Brad, Michael O. Emerson, and Korie L. Edwards. 2005. *Against all odds: The struggle of racial integration in religious organizations.* New York University Press.

Churchill, Ward. 1998. *A little matter of genocide: Holocaust and denial in the Americas, 1492 to the present.* City Lights.

Clark, Christine, and James O'Donnell, eds. 1999. *Becoming and unbecoming white: owning and disowning a racial identity.* Bergin & Garvey.

Cohen, E. G. 1984. The desegregated school: Problems in status, power, and interethnic climate. In *Groups in contact: The psychology of desegregation*, ed. N. Miller and M. B. Brewer. Academic Press.

Cole, Steward G., and Mildred W. Cole. 1954. *Minorities and the American promise.* Harper & Brothers.

Cone, James H. 1999. *Risks of faith: The emergence of a black theology of liberation, 1968–1998.* Beacon.

Connerly, Ward. 2000. *Creating equal: My fight against race preferences.* Encounter Books.

Connor, John W. 1974. Acculturation of family continuities in three generations of Japanese Americans. *Journal of Marriage and Family* 36(1):159–65.

Cornell, Drucilla. 1998. *At the heart of freedom: Feminism, sex, and equality.* Princeton University Press.

Cox, Oliver C. 2001. *Race: A study in social dynamics.* Monthly Review Press.

Cox, Taylor. 2004. Problems with research by organizational scholars on issues of race and ethnicity. *Journal of Applied Behavioral Science* 40(2):124–45.

Crenshaw, Kimberle, Neil Gotanda, Gary Peller, and Kendall Thomas, eds. 1995. *Critical race theory: The key writings that formed the movement.* The New Press.

D'souza, Dinesh. 1996. *The end of racism: Principles for a multiracial society.* Free Press.

Dahrendorf, Ralf. 1959. *Class and class conflict in industrial society.* Stanford University Press.

Dalmage, Heather M. 2000. *Tripping on the color line.* Rutgers University Press.

Darity, William Jr. 2008. Forty acres and a mule in the 21st century. *Social Science Quarterly* 89(3):656–64.

———, and Dania Frank. 2003. The economics of reparations. *American Economic Review* 93(2):326–29.

Davis, Robert C., and Edna Erez. 1998. *Immigrant population as victims: Toward a multicultural criminal justice system.* National Institute of Justice.

Delgado, Richard, and Jean Stefancic, eds. 2000. *Critical race theory: The cutting edge.* 2nd ed. Temple University Press.

Derman-Sparks, Louise, and Carol B. Phillips. 1997. *Teaching/learning anti-racism.* Teachers College Press.

DeWitt, John L. 1942. Final recommendation of cCommanding general, Western Defense Command and Fourth Army.

DeYmaz, Mark. 2007. *Building a healthy multi-ethnic church.* John Wiley.

DeYoung, Curtiss, Michael O. Emerson, George Yancey, and Karen Chai. 2003. *United by faith: The multiracial congregation as an answer to the problem of race.* Oxford University Press.

Dixon, Jeffrey C., and Michael S. Rosenbaum. 2004. Nice to know you? Testing contact, cultural and group threat theories of anti-black and anti-Hispanic stereotypes. *Social Science Quarterly* 85(2):257–80.

Dovidio, John, and Samuel L. Gaertner. 1998. On the nature of contemporary prejudice: The causes, consequences, and challenges of aversive racism. In *Confronting racism: The problem and the response*, ed. Jennifer Eberharett and Susan T. Fiske, 3–32. Sage.

Dyer, Richard. 1997. *White.* Routledge.

Dyson, Michael. 1996. *Race rules: Navigating the color line.* Addison Wesley Longman.

———. 2000. *I may not get there with you: The true Martin Luther King, Jr.* Free Press.

Eastland, Terry. 1997. *Ending affirmative action: The case for colorblind justice.* Basic Books.

Ecklund, Elaine Howard. 2005. Models of civic responsibility: Korean Americans in congregations with different ethnic compositions. *Journal for the Scientific Study of Religion* 44:15–28.

———. 2006. *Korean American evangelicals: New models for civic life.* Oxford University Press.

Editorial. 2000. Racial profiling study needs a push. *St. Petersburg Times*, September 28.

Edwards, Korie L. 2008. *The elusive dream: The power of race in interracial churches*. Oxford University Press.

Elashmawi, Farid, and Philip Harris. 1998. *Multicultural management 2000: Essential cultural insights for global business success*. Butterworth-Heinemann.

Elder, Larry. 2002. *Showdown: Confronting bias, lies, and the special interest that divide America*. St. Martin's Press.

Elkin, Stanley M. 1976. *Slavery: A problem in American institutional and intellectual life*. University of Chicago Press.

Ellison, Christopher, and Daniel Powers. 1994. The contact hypothesis and racial attitudes among black Americans. *Social Science Quarterly* 75(2):385–400.

Emerson, Michael O. 2006. *People of the dream: Multiracial congregations in the United States*. Princeton University Press.

———, and Christian Smith. 2000. *Divided by faith: Evangelical religion and the problem of race in America*. Oxford University Press.

———, and George Yancey. 2008. African Americans in interracial congregations: An analysis of demographics, social networks, and social attitudes. *Review of Religious Research* 49:301–18.

Enrile, Annalisa, and Pauline T. Agbayani. 2007. Differences in attitudes towards women among three groups of Filipinos: Filipinos in the Philippines, Filipino American immigrants, and U.S.-born Filipino Americans. *Journal of Ethnic & Cultural Diversity in Social Work* 16(1, 2):1–25.

Eschbach, Karl. 1995. The enduring and vanishing American Indian: American Indian population growth and intermarriage in 1990. *Ethnic and Racial Studies* 18:89–108.

Fan, Hong. 1997. *Footbinding, feminism and freedom: The liberation of women's bodies in modern China*. Routledge.

Feagin, Joe R. 2000. *Racist America: Roots, current realities, and future reparations*. Routledge.

———, and Hernan Vera. 2000. *White racism: The basics*. Routledge.

Feagin, Joseph. 2005. *The many costs of racism*. Rowman & Littlefield.

Federici, Silvia, ed. 1995. *Enduring western civilization: The construction of the concept of western civilization and its Others*. Praeger.

Fekete, Liz. 2004. Anti-Muslim racism and the European security state. *Race and Class* 46(1):3–29.

Feng, Yi, and Paul J. Zak. 1999. The determinants of democratic transitions. *Journal of Conflict Resolution* 43(2):162–77.

Fetto, John. 2000. Interracial friendships slip? *American Demographics* 22(1):23.

Fetzer, Joel S., and J. Christopher Soper. 2005. *Muslims and the state in Britain, France, and Germany*. Cambridge University Press.

Flagg, Barbara. 1993. Was blind, but now I see: White race consciousness and the requirement of discriminatory intent. *Michigan Law Review* 91:953.

Forman, Tyrone A. 2004. Colorblind racism and racial indifference: The role of racial apathy in facilitating enduring inequalities. In *The Changing Terrain of Race and Ethnicity*, ed. Maria Krysan and Amanda Lewis, 43–66. Russell Sage Foundation.

———, and Amanda E. Lewis. 2006. Racial apathy and Hurricane Katrina: The social anatomy of prejudice in the post–civil rights era. *Du Bois Review* 3:175–202.

Fredrickson, George M. 1971. *The black image in the white mind*. Harper & Row.

Fuchs, Lawrence H. 1995. *The American kaleidoscope: Race, ethnicity, and the civic culture*. Wesleyan University Press.

Gaertner, Samuel L., and John Dovidio. 1986. The aversive form of racism. In *Prejudice, discrimination, and racism: Theory and research*, ed. John Dovidio and Samuel L. Gaertner. Academic Press.

Gallagher, Charles A. 2004a. Racial redistricting: Expanding the boundaries of whiteness. In *The politics of multiracialism: Challenging racial thinking*, ed. Robert W. Hefner, 59–76. State University of New York.

———. 2004b. Ten simple things you can do to improve race relations. In *Rethinking the color line: Readings in race and ethnicity*, ed. Charles A. Gallagher, 582–85. McGraw Hill.

George, Douglas, and George Yancey. 2009. Forming a more perfect union: Racial perceptions of unity and division in the United States. *Sociological Focus:1–19*.

Gibeaut, John. 1999. Profiling: Marked for humiliation. *American Bar Association Journal* February: 46–47.

Gilens, Martin. 1995. Racial attitudes and opposition to welfare. *Journal of Politics* 57(4):994–1014.

Gleason, Philip. 1980. American identity and Americanization. In *Harvard Encyclopedia of American Ethnic Groups*, ed. Stephan Thernstrom, 31–58. Belknap.

Gordon, Milton M. 1964. *Assimilation in American life*. Oxford University Press.

Greene, Helen Taylor. 1997. Teaching delinquency: Using research by black scholars in undergraduate courses. *Teaching Sociology* 25:57–64.

Guinier, Lani, and Gerald Torres. 2003. *The miner's canary: Enlisting race, resisting power, transforming democracy*. Harvard University Press.

Hacker, Andrew. 1995. *Two nations: Black and white, separate, hostile, and unequal*. Ballantine.

Hall, Edward T., and Mildred R. Hall. 1990. *Understanding cultural differences*. Intercultural Press.

Handlin, Oscar. 1957. *Race and nationality in American life*. Doubleday Anchor Books.

Harris, Andrea L. 2003. Generation X X: The identity politics of Generation X. In *GenXegesis: Essays on alternative youth (sub)culture*, ed. John M. Ulrich, and Andrea L. Harris, 268–94. University of Wisconsin Press.

Harris, David A. 1999. Driving while black: Racial profiling on our nation's highways. American Civil Liberties Union.

———. 2003. *Profiles in injustice: Why racial profiling cannot work.* W. W. Norton.

Hartigan, John Jr. 1999. *Racial situations: Class predicaments of whiteness in Detroit.* Princeton University Press.

Heaton, Tim B., and Stan L. Albrecht. 1996. The changing patterns of inter-racial marriage. *Social Biology* 43(3–4):203–17.

Hechter, Michael. 1987. *Principles of social solidarity.* University of California Press.

Hewstone, Miles. 1986. Contact is not enough: An intergroup perspective on the contact hypothesis. In *Contact and conflict in intergroup encounters,* ed. Miles Hewstone and Rupert Brown, 1–44. Basil Blackwell.

Higham, John. 2001. *Hanging together: Unity and diversity in American culture.* Yale University Press.

Hirschman, C. 1983. America's melting pot reconsidered. In *Annual Review of Sociology,* ed. R. H. Turner. 397–423.

Hirschmann, Nancy J. 2002. *The subject of liberty: Toward a feminist theory of freedom.* Princeton University Press.

Hochschild, Jennifer L. 1995. *Facing Up to the American dream: Race, class and the soul of the nation.* Princeton University Press.

Hofstede, Geert. 1980. *Culture's consequences.* Sage.

Hogg, Michael A., and Dominic Abrams. 1988. *Social identifications: A social psychology of intergroup relations and group processes.* Rutledge.

Hopkins, Dwight N. 2000. *Down, up and over: Slave religion and black theology.* Augsburg Fortress.

Horowitz, David. 2002. *Uncivil wars: The controversy over reparations for slavery.* Encounter Books.

———, and Jamie Glazov. 2003. *Left illusions: An intellectual odyssey.* Spence.

Huddy, Leonie, and David O. Sears. 1990. Qualified public support for bilingual education: Some policy implications. *Annals of the American Academy of Political and Social Science* 508:119–34.

Hughes, Michael, and David H. Demo. 1989. Self-perceptions of black Americans: Personal self-esteem, racial self-esteem, and personal efficacy. *American Journal of Sociology* 95:132–59.

Human Rights Watch. 2001. *An approach to reparations.* Human Rights Watch.

Hwang, Sean-Shong, Rogelio Saenz, and Benigno E. Aguirre. 1995. The SES selectivity of interracially married Asians. *International Migration Review* 29 (2):469–91.

Ibarra, Robert A. 1999. Multicontextuality: A new perspective on minority underrepresentation in SEM academic fields. *Research News on Minority Graduate Education* 1(3):1-9.

Ignatiev, Noel. 1997. Treason to whiteness is loyalty to humanity: An interview with Noel Ignatiev of *Race Traitor Magazine.* In *Critical white studies: Looking behind the mirror,* ed. Richard Delgado and Jean Stefancic, 607–12. Temple University Press.

———, and John Garvey, eds. 1996. *Race traitor.* Routledge.

Irvine, S. 1973. Racial attitudes of American ministers. In *Annual meeting of the American psychological association*. American Psychological Association.

Jackman, Mary, and Marie Crane. 1986. Some of my best friends are black . . . : Interracial friendship and whites' racial Attitudes. *Public Opinion Quarterly* 50:459–86.

Johnson, Kirk. 1993. Rich, but not in history, Connecticut Pequots sponsor cultural powwow. *New York Times*, September 19.

Jordan, Winthrop D. 1968. *White over black*. Penguin.

Joyner, Kara, and Grace Kao. 2000. School racial composition and adolescent racial homophily. *Social Science Quarterly* 81(3):810–25.

Kalmijn, Matthijs. 1994. Assortive mating by cultural and economic occupational status. *American Journal of Sociology* 100:422–452.

Karatnycky, Adrian. 2002. Muslim countries and the democracy gap. *Journal of Democracy* 13(1):99–112.

Katz, Judith. 2003. *White awareness: A handbook for anti-racism training*. University of Oklahoma Press.

Killian, Kyle D. 2001. Reconstituting racial histories and identities: The narratives of interracial couples. *Journal of marital and family therapy* 27(1):27–42.

Kim, Uichol. 1995. *Individualism and collectivism: A psychological, cultural and ecological analysis*. Nordic Institute of Asian Studies.

Kinder, Donald R., and Lynn M. Sanders. 1981. *Divided by color: Racial politics and democratic ideals*. University of Chicago Press.

King, Martin Luther. 1958. *Stride towards freedom: The Montgomery story*. Harper.

———. 2003. Letter from a Birmingham jail. In *Liberating faith: Religious voices for justice, peace, and ecological wisdom*, ed. Roger S. Gottlieb, 177–187. Rowman & Littlefield.

King, Richard H. 1996. *Civil rights and the idea of freedom*. University of Georgia Press.

Kivel, Paul. 2002. *Uprooting racism: How white people can work for racial justice*. New Society.

Kluegel, James R. 1990. Trends in whites' explanation of the black–white gap in socioeconomic status, 1977–1989. *American Sociological Review* 55:512–25.

Knowles, John, Nicola Persico, and Todd Petra. 2001. Racial bias in motor-vehicle searches: Theory and evidence. *Journal of Political Economy* 109 (1):203–29.

Korgen, Kathleen Odell. 2002. *Crossing the racial divide: Close friendships between black and white Americans*. Praeger.

Korstad, Robert, and Nelson Lichtenstein. 1988. Opportunities found and lost: Labor, radicals, and the early civil rights movement. *Journal of American History* 75(3):786–811.

Krysan, Maria. 2002. Whites who say they flee: Who are they, and why would they leave? *Demography* 39(4):675–96.

Ladson-Billings, Gloria, ed. 2003. *Critical race theory perspectives on the social studies: The profession, policies, and curriculum*. Information Age.

Lawson, Steven F. 1991. Freedom then, freedom now: The historiography of the civil rights movement. *American Historical Review* 96(2):456–71.

Lee, Robert. 1992. Burn Out "melting pot" in an age of cultural diversity. *Asian Week* 13(42):19.

Lee, Robert G. 1999. *Orientals: Asian Americans in popular culture*. Temple University Press.

Lee, Wanda M. L. 1999. *Introduction to multicultural counseling*. Routledge.

Levine, Lawrence W. 1996. *The opening of the American mind*. Beacon.

Lewis, Amanda E. 2004. "What group?" Studying whites and whiteness in the era of "color-blindness." *Sociological Theory* 22:623–46.

Lewis, Denise C. 2008. Types, meanings and ambivalence in intergenerational exchanges among Cambodian refugee families in the United States. *Ageing and Society* 28(5):693–715.

Li, Qiong, and Marilynn B. Brewer. 2004. What does it mean to be an American? Patriotism, nationalism, and American identity after 9/11. *Political Psychology* 25(5):727–39.

Lio, Shoon, Scott Melzer, and Ellen Reese. 2008. Constructing threat and appropriating "civil rights": Rhetorical strategies of gun rights and English-only leaders. *Symbolic Interaction* 31(1):5–31.

Lipset, Seymour M. 1991. American exceptionalism reaffirmed. In *Is America different?: A new look at American exceptionalism*, ed. Byron E. Shafer. Oxford University Press.

Lipsitz, George. 1995. The possessive investment in whiteness: Racialized social democracy and the "white' problem in American studies." *American Quarterly* 47:369–87.

Luke, Carmen, and Allan Luke. 1998. Interracial families: Difference within difference. *Ethnic and Racial Studies* 21(4):728–53.

Manchester-Boddy, E. 1970. *Japanese in America*. R & E Research Associates.

Manning, Marable. 2000. *How capitalism underdeveloped black America: Problems in race, political economy, and society*. South End Press.

Marti, Gerardo. 2005. *A mosaic of believers: Diversity and innovation in a multiethnic church*. Indiana University Press.

Massey, Douglas S., and Nancy Denton. 1996. *American apartheid: Segregation and the making of the underclass*. Harvard University Press.

McConahay, John B. 1986. Modern racism, ambivalence, and the modern racism scale. In *Prejudice, discrimination, and racism: Theory and research*, ed. John Dovidio and Samuel L. Gaertner, 91–125. Academic Press.

———., and J. C. Hough Jr. 1976. Symbolic Racism. *Journal of Social Issues* 32(1):23–45.

McGavran, Donald A. 1990. *Understanding church growth*. 3rd ed. William B. Eerdmans.

McGroarty, Mary. 1992. The Societal context of bilingual education. *Educational Researcher* 21(2):7–9, 24.

McIntosh, Peggy. 2002. White privilege: Unpacking the invisible knapsack. In *White privilege: Essential readings on the other side of racism*, ed. Paula S. Rothenberg, 97–102. Worth.

McRoy, Ruth G., and Louis A. Zurcher. 1983. *Transracial and inracial adoptees: The adolescent years*. Thomas.

McWhorter, John. 2001. *Losing the race: Self-sabotage in black America*. Perennial.

———. 2006. Don't do me any favors: A black case against race preferences. In *Annual editions 2005–2006 race and ethnic relations*, ed. John A. Kromskowski, 219–24. McGraw Hill.

Mead, George Herbert. 1934. *Mind, self and society*. University of Chicago Press.

Mechanic, David. 2005. Policy challenges in addressing racial disparities and improving population health. *Health Affairs* 24(2):335–38.

Miner, Barbara. 2004. Taking multicultural, antiracist education seriously: An interview with Enid Lee. In *Race, class and gender: An anthology*, ed. Margaret L. Andersen and Patricia H. Collins, 348–53. Wadsworth.

Miracle, A. W. 1981. Factors affecting interracial cooperation: A case study of a high school football team. *Human Organization* 40:150–54.

Mkandelbaum, D. G. 1952. *Soldier groups and negro soldiers*. University of California Press.

Moorehead, Monica. 2002. Reparations and black liberation. *Workers World Newspaper* 44(22):1, 7.

Morning, Ann. 2000. Counting on the color line: Socioeconomic status of multiracial Americans. Paper presented at the annual conference of the *Population Association of America*.

Moskos, Charles C., and John S. Butler. 1996. *All that we can be: Black leadership and racial integration the Army way*. Basic Books.

Moynihan, Daniel P. 1965. *The negro family*. U.S. Department of Labor.

Myers, David G. 1993. *Social psychology*. 4th ed. McGraw-Hill.

Myrdal, Gunnar. 1944. *An American dilemma: The negro problem and American democracy*. Harper.

Nagel, Joane, and C. Matthew Snipp. 1993. Ethnic reorganization: American Indian social, economic, political, and cultural strategies for survival. *Ethnic and Racial Studies* April: 203–35.

Newman, W. M. 1973. *American pluralism: A study of minority groups and social theory*. Harper & Row.

Niebuhr, Reinhold. 1932. *Moral man and immoral society: A study in ethics and politics.*. Scribner's.

Nielsen, Jorgen S. 1999. *Towards a European Islam*. Macmillan.

O'Brien, Eileen. 2001. *Whites confront racism: Antiracists and their path to action*. Rowman & Littlefield.

O'Neill, Terry. 2002. Introduction. In *The Indian reservation system*, ed. Terry O'Neill 3–16. Greenhaven.

Ogbu, John. 1978. *Minority education and caste*. Academic Press.

Oliver, Melvin L., and Thomas M. Shapiro. 1995. *Black wealth/white wealth: A new perspective on racial inequality*. Routledge.

Orfield, Gary, and Susan Eaton. 1996. *Dismantling desegregation: The quiet reversal of Brown v. Board of Education*. New Press.

Ortner, Sherry B. 1998. Generation X: Anthropology in a media-saturated world. *Cultural Anthropology* 13(3):414–40.

Parekh, Bhikhu. 2000. *Rethinking multiculturalism: Cultural diversity and political theory*. Harvard University Press.

Parker, James H. 1968. The interaction of negroes and whites in an integrated church setting. *Social Forces* 46 (March): 359–66.

Pedraza, Silvia. 2000. Beyond black and white: Latinos and social science research on immigration, race, and ethnicity in America. *Social Science History* 24(4):697–726.

Peffley, Mark, Jon Hurwitz, and Paul M. Sniderman. 1997. Racial stereotypes and whites' political views of blacks in then context of welfare and crime. *American Journal of Political Science* 41(1):30–60.

Perkins, Spencer, and Chris Rice. 2000. *More than equals: Racial healing for the sake of the gospel*. InterVarsity.

Pettigrew, Thomas F. 1998. Intergroup contact theory. *Annual Review of Psychology* 49:65–85.

———., and L. R. Tropp. 2000. Does intergroup contact reduce prejudice? Recent meta-analytic findings. In *Reducing prejudice and discrimination*, ed. S. Oskamp, 93-114. Lawrence Erlbaum.

Pettigrew, Thomas F. 1989. The nature of modern racism in the United States. *Revue Internationale de Psychologie Sociale* 2:291–303.

Pincus, Fred L. 1996. Test of affirmative action knowledge. *Current World Leaders International* 39:94–104.

Pinkney, Alphonso. 2000. *Black Americans*. Prentice-Hall.

Pocock, Michael, and Joseph Henriques. 2002. *Cultural change and your church: Helping your church thrive in a diverse society*. Baker Book House.

Poncini, Gina. 2004. *Discursive strategies in multicultural business meetings*. Peter Lang.

Ponterotto, Joseph G., J. Manuel Casas, Lisa A. Suzuki, and Charlene M. Alexander. 2001. *Handbook of multicultural counseling*. Sage.

Pope-Davis, Donald, and Hardin L. K. Coleman. 2000. *The intersection of race, class, and gender: Implications for multicultural counseling*. Sage.

Portes, Alejandro, and Min Zhou. 1994. Should immigrants assimilate? *The Public Interest* 116 (Summer): 18–33.

Qian, Zhenchao. 1999. Who intermarries? Education, nativity, region, and interracial marriage, 1980 and 1990. *Journal of Comparative Family Studies* 30(4):579–97.

Ramos-Sanchez, Lucila, and Donald R. Atkinson. 2009. The relationships between Mexican American acculturation, cultural values, gender, and help-seeking intentions. *Journal of Counseling & Development* 87:62–71.

Rath, Jan, Rinus Penninx, Kees Groenendijk, and Meyer Astrid. 2001. *Western Europe and its Islam.* Brill.

Ravitch, Diane. 1994. Our pluralistic common culture. In *Civil rights and social wrongs: Black–white relations since World War II,* ed. John Higham. Pennsylvania State University Press.

Rice, Chris. 2003. *Grace matters: A memoir of faith, friendship, and hope in the heart of the South.* Jossey-Bass.

Ricento, Thomas. 2003. The discursive construction of Americanism. *Discourse & Society* 14(5):611–37.

Ringer, Benjamin B. 1983. *We the People and others: Duality and America's treatment of its racial minorities.* Tavistock.

Roberts, J. Deotis. 2005. *Liberation and reconciliation: A black theology.* Westminister John Knox Press.

Robinson, Randall. 2000. *The debt: What America owes to blacks.* Penguin Putman.

Root, Maria P. P. 2001. *Love's revolution: Interracial marriage.* Temple University Press.

Rosenblatt, Paul C., Terri A. Karis, and Richard D. Powell. 1995. *Multiracial couples: Black and white voices.* Sage.

Rosenthal, Steven J. 1980. Symbolic racism and desegregation: Divergent attitudes and perceptions of black and white university students. *Phylon* 41(3):257–66.

Royster, Deirdre A. 2003. *Race and the invisible hand: How white networks exclude black men from blue-collar jobs.* University of California Press.

Ryan, William. 1976. *Blaming the victim.* Random House.

Rytina, Steve L. 1992. Sealing the intergenerational continuity of occupation: Is occupational inheritance ascriptive after all. *American Journal of Sociology* 97:1658–88.

Sacks, Peter. 1996. *Generation X goes to college: An eye-opening account of teaching in postmodern America.* Open Court.

Salzberger, Ronald, and Mary C. Turck. 2004. *Reparations for slavery: A reader.* Rowman & Littlefield.

Schildkraut, Deborah J. 2002. The more things change . . . American identity and mass and elite responses to 9/11. *Political Psychology* 23(3):511–35.

Schlesinger, Arthur M. Jr. 1992. *The disuniting of America: Reflections on a multicultural society.* W. W. Norton.

Schreiber, Alfred L., and Barry Lenson. 2000. *Multicultural marketing.* McGraw-Hill.

Schuman, Howard, Charlotte Steeh, Lawrence Bobo, and Maria Krysan. 1997. *Racial attitudes in America: Trends and interpretations.* Harvard University Press.

Sears, David O. 1988. Symbolic Racism. In *Eliminating racism,* ed. Phyllis A. Katz, and Dalmas A. Taylor, 53–84. Plenum.

Shadid, W., and P. S. van Koningsveld. 2005. Muslim dress in Europe: Debates on the headscarf. *Journal of Islamic Studies* 16(1):35–61.

Sidanius, Jim, Pam Singh, John J. Hetts, and Chris Federico. 2000. It's not affirmative action, it's the blacks." In *Racialized politics: The debate about racism in America*, ed. David O. Sears, Jim Sidanius, and Lawrence Bobo, 191–235. University of Chicago Press.

Simms, Rupe. 2001. Black theology, a weapon in the struggle for freedom: A Gramscian analysis. *Race and Society* 2(2):165–93.

Singh, Robert. 1999. Gun politics in America: Continuity and change. *Parliamentary Affairs* 52(1):1–18.

Sniderman, Paul M., and Thomas Piazza. 1993. *The scar of race*. Harvard University Press.

Song, Sarah. 2009. What does it mean to be an American. *Daedalus* 138(2):31–40.

Spickard, Paul. 1989. *Mixed blood: Intermarriage and ethnic identity in twentieth-century America*. Sage.

Spiro, Peter J. 2008. *Beyond citizenship: American identity after globalization*. Oxford University Press.

St. John, Nancy H. 1975. *School desegregation outcomes for children*. Wiley.

Steele, Shelby. 1990. *The content of our character: A new vision of race in America*. St. Martin's Press.

———. 1994. *A dream deferred: The second betrayal of black freedom*. Harper Collins.

Stein, Robert M., Stephanie Shirley Post, and Allison L. Rinden. 2000. Reconciling context and contact effects on racial attitudes. *Political Research Quarterly* 53(2):285–303.

Stephan, W. G. 1987. The contact hypothesis in intergroup relations. In *Review of personality and social psychology: Group processes and intergroup relations*, ed. C. Hendrick, 13–40. Sage.

Sumner, William G. 1906. *Folkways*. Ginn.

Taifel, Henri. 1981. *Human groups and social categories*. Cambridge University Press.

Tarver, Marsha, Steve Walker, and Harvey Wallace. 2002. *Multicultural issues in the criminal justice system*. Allyn & Bacon.

Tate, W. F. 1996. Critical Race Theory and Education: History, Theory, and Implications. *Review of Research in Education* 22:195–247.

Thomas, Clarence. 1997. No room at the inn: The loneliness of the black conservative. In *Black and right: The bold new voice of black conservatives in America*, ed. Stan Faryna, Brad Stetson, and Joseph G. Conti, 3–14. Praeger.

Thomas, James M., and David L. Brunsma. 2008. Bringing down the house: Reparations, universal morality, human rights and social justice. In *Globalization and America: Race, human rights, and inequality*, ed. Angela J. Hattery, David G. Embrick, and Earl Smith, 65–81. Rowman & Littlefield.

Thomson, Irene Taviss. 1989. The transformation of the social bond: Images of individualism in the 1920s versus the 1970s. *Social Forces* 67(4):851–70.

Tibi, Bassam. 2002. Muslim migrants in Europe: Between Euro-Islam and ghettoization. In *Muslim Europe or Euro-Islam: Politics, culture, and citizenship in the age of globalization*, ed. Nezar AlSayyad and Manuel Castells, 31–52. Lexington Books.

Tuch, Steven A., and Michael Hughes. 1996. Whites' racial policy attitudes. *Social Science Quarterly* 77(4):723–45.

Tucker, M. Belinda, and Claudia Mitchell-Kernan. 1990. New trends in black American interracial marriage: The social structural context. *Journal of Marriage and the Family* 52:209–18.

Twine, France Winddance. 1997. Brown-skinned white girls: Class, culture, and the construction of white identity in suburban communities. In *Displacing whiteness: Essays in social and cultural criticism*, ed. Ruth Frankenberg, 214-243. Duke University Press.

Utter, Glenn H., and James L. True. 2000. The evolving gun culture in America. *Journal of American Culture* 23(2):67–79.

Wachtel, Paul L. 1999. *Race in the mind of America: Breaking the vicious cycle between blacks and whites.* Routledge.

Wagner, C. Peter. 1979. *Our kind of people: The ethical dimensions of church growth in America.* John Knox.

———. 1996. *The healthy church: Avoiding and curing the 9 diseases that can afflict any church.* Regal Books.

Warren, Earl. 1942. Japanese Americans pose a serious threat to national security. 11010–18.

Washburn, Wilcomb E. 1975. *The Indian in America.* Harper & Row.

Waters, Mary C. 1990. *Ethnic options: Choosing identities in America.* University of California Press.

———. 1999. *Black identities: West Indian immigrant dreams and American realities.* Russell Sage Foundation.

West, Cornel. 2001. *Race matters.* Vintage Books.

Westley, Robert. 2003. Many billions gone: Is it time to reconsider the case for black reparations? In *Should America pay? Slavery and the raging debate on reparations*, ed. Raymond Winbush, 109-134. Amistad.

Wildman, Stephanie M., and Adrienne D. Davis. 2002. Making systems of privilege visible. In *White privilege: Essential readings on the other side of racism*, ed. Paula S. Rothenberg, 89–95. Worth.

Williams, Armstrong. 2003. Presumed victims. In *Should American pay? Slavery and the raging debate on reparations*, ed. Raymond A. Wimbush, 165–71. HarperCollins.

Williams, Robin M. 1970. *American society: A sociological interpretation.* 3rd ed. Alfred A. Knopf.

Wilson, Sandra. 2001. *Hurt people hurt people.* Discovery House.

Wilson, Thomas C. 1996. Cohort and prejudice: Whites' attitudes toward blacks, Hispanics, Jews, and Asians. *Public Opinion Quarterly* 60(2):253–74.

Wilson, William J. 1973. *Power, racism and privilege: Race relations in theoretical and sociohistorical perspectives.* Free Press.

———. 1980. *The declining significance of race.* University of Chicago Press.

———. 1987. *The truly disadvantaged.* University of Chicago Press.

Wilson, Woodrow. 1924. *The messages and papers of Woodrow Wilson.* Review of Reviews Corporation.

———. 1931. *America's greatness: Gathered from the works of Woodrow Wilson.* Wm. H. Wise.

Winfield, Betty H., Takeya Mizuno, and Christopher E. Beaudoin. 2000. Confucianism, collectivism and constitutions: Press systems in China and Japan. *Communications Law and Policy* 5:323–47.

Wise, Tim. 2002. Membership has its privileges: Thoughts on acknowledging and challenging whiteness. In *White privilege: Essential readings on the other side of racism,* ed. Paula S. Rothenberg, 133-136. Worth.

———. 2005. *White like me: Reflections on race from a privileged son.* Soft Skull.

Yancey, George. 1999. An examination of effects of residential and church integration upon racial attitudes of whites. *Sociological Perspectives* 42 (2):279–304.

———. 2001. Racial attitudes: Differences in racial attitudes of people attending multiracial and uniracial congregations. *Research in the Social Scientific Study of Religion* 12:185–206.

———. 2003a. *One body, one spirit: Principles of successful multiracial churches.* InterVarsity.

———. 2003b. *Who is white?: Latinos, Asians, and the new black/nonblack divide.* Lynne Rienner.

———. 2007a. Experiencing racism: Differences in the experiences of whites married to blacks and non-black racial minorities. *Journal of Comparative Family Studies* 38(2):197–213.

———. 2007b. *Interracial contact and social change.* Lynne Rienner.

Zinn, Howard, and Donaldo Macedo. 2004. *Howard Zinn on democratic Education.* Paradigm.

INDEX

9 780199 742691